Lucky 13

solitaire games for kids

♠ ♥ ♣ ♦ ♠ ♥ ♣ ♦

Michael Street

illustrated by Alan Tiegreen

SEA STAR BOOKS
NEW YORK

For my family
—M.S.

Text copyright © 2001 by Michael Street
Illustrations copyright © 2001 by Alan Tiegreen
Diagrams copyright © 2001 by SeaStar Books

SEASTAR BOOKS
A division of NORTH-SOUTH BOOKS INC.

First published in the United States by SeaStar Books, a division of North-South Books Inc., New York.
Published simultaneously in Great Britain, Canada, Australia, and New Zealand by North-South Books,
an imprint of Nord-Süd Verlag AG, Gossau Zürich, Switzerland.

A CIP catalogue record is available from The British Library.

Library of Congress Cataloging-in-Publication Data
Street, Michael.
Lucky 13: solitaire games for kids/by Michael Street; illustrated by Alan Tiegreen.
p. cm.
1. Solitaire (Game)—Juvenile literature. [1. Solitaire (Game) 2. Games.] I. Tiegreen, Alan, ill. II. Title.
GV 1261 .S77 2001
795.4'3—dc21
00-63764

The artwork for this book was prepared by using pen and ink.

ISBN 1-58717-013-2 (reinforced trade binding)
1 3 5 7 9 RT 10 8 6 4 2
ISBN 1-58717-014-0 (paperback binding)
1 3 5 7 9 PB 10 8 6 4 2

Printed in the U.S.A.

For more information about our books, and the authors and artists who create them,
visit our web site: www.northsouth.com

Contents

♠ ♥ ♣ ♦ ♠ ♥ ♣ ♦

Introduction

♠ ♥ ♣ ♦ ♠ ♥ ♣ ♦

We've all had the experience of wanting to play a game but having no one to play with. Mom and Dad are at work, your best friend is sick with the measles, and your little sister can't even talk yet, let alone play a game with you. But all you need is a pack of cards for hours of fun—if you know how to play solitaire.

Solitaire was invented almost three hundred years ago, at a time when whist, a card game requiring four players, was all the rage in France. If someone wanted to play whist, but didn't have three other people, he would simply deal four hands and play each hand himself, imagining how a real game might have gone. The French called this practice *solitaire*.

Napoleon Bonaparte, the famous French general and emperor, is said to have played a lot of solitaire, and many early solitaire games were named after him. Whether or not Napoleon invented or actually played solitaire, it is easy to imagine this brilliant military man frowning over a table full of cards. The best kinds of solitaire require you to think through your moves carefully, just like a great general plans out his strategy before an important battle.

Before you get started, there are some important terms and some basic strategies to solitaire that you'll need to know. Each game will use these terms, but you can always refer to the glossary at the back of the book if you forget what a word means.

rank and suit of cards

Cards are **ranked** from ace to king. The ace is the lowest card and the king is the highest. The numbered cards follow the ace in rising order, so that a five is higher than a four, and a ten is higher than a nine. Just above the ten is the jack, followed by the queen, and then the king. The jack, queen, and king are called **face cards**, since they are the only cards with faces. For most number-based games, aces are counted as ones, jacks as elevens, queens as twelves, and kings as thirteens.

Cards come in four **suits**—hearts, diamonds, clubs, and spades. While no suit ranks above or below the other in solitaire, it's important to notice that two suits (hearts and diamonds) are red and the other two (clubs and spades) are black.

building

The heart of all solitaire games is **building**, placing one card on another in a certain sequence, usually according to the rank of the cards. A sequence of two or more cards properly built up or down is called a **build**. In almost every game, only the **top card** of a build—the card appearing at the bottom of a row or column, with no cards played on it—can be played upon.

Building up means that you can only put a card on another card one rank *below* it, so that a four must be played on a three or a king on a queen. A pile of thirteen cards built up will have the lowest card (ace) on the bottom and the highest card (king) on the top.

Building down means that you can only put a card on another card one rank *higher* than it, so that a ten is played on a jack or a seven on an eight. A pile of thirteen cards built down will have the highest card (king) on the bottom and the lowest card (ace) on the top.

building   building
  up   down

building by suit

Most of the time, you cannot build up by putting just any four on any three. If a game says that you have to **build by suit,** then you can only place a card on another card of the same suit—a four of diamonds on the three of diamonds, for example. This is the hardest way to build, since each card can only be placed on one other card. The **foundations** (see page 11) are usually built by suit.

building by color

Another way to build is **building by color,** either the same color (red on red and black on black) or alternate colors (red on black and black on red). So **building up by alternate colors** means that a jack of hearts (red) can only be played on a ten of spades or clubs (both black suits). Or you can **build down by the same color.** Using the same example, the red jack of hearts would be played on a queen of diamonds or hearts. Building by color, however, is almost always done in alternate colors.

moving a build

In many games, a complete or partial build may be moved from one pile to another to make a longer build. To play a build onto another build or card, pick up the whole column of cards in the build (but not the face-down cards underneath, if there are any) and place the column on the top card of any other pile. Remember that the top card of a build is the card at the bottom of the column, the only card without another card on top of it. The new column of cards created when you do this should follow the building rules of the game, building up or down in the proper suit or color, with no missing or repeated ranks.

Some games allow you to move only **completed builds,** which means that a whole column of cards must be moved and not just a part of that column. Others allow you to move **partial builds** containing two or more consecutive cards from the build, so that you can break a build at a certain point in order to play a card that you need. For example, you might need a six of diamonds to continue a foundation, but it's covered by the other cards in its build. Then you notice the six of hearts at the bottom of another pile. If you're allowed to move partial builds, take the cards below the six of diamonds and place them on the six of hearts. The six of diamonds is now available for you to use.

MOVING A COMPLETE BUILD

correct

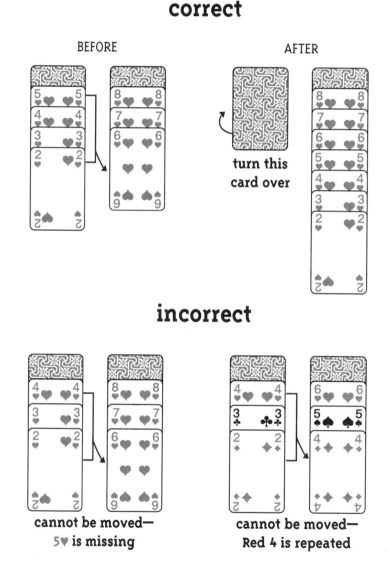

incorrect

cannot be moved—
5♥ is missing

cannot be moved—
Red 4 is repeated

MOVING A PARTIAL BUILD

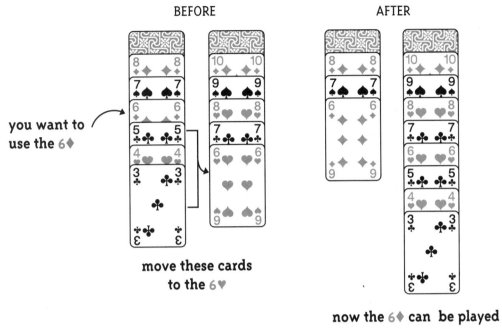

BEFORE   AFTER

you want to
use the 6♦

move these cards
to the 6♥

now the 6♦ can be played
to a foundation

layout

Most solitaire games begin when you deal cards in a certain way into piles, rows, or columns. This is called the **layout.** These cards are dealt either face up or face down; each game will tell you which way to deal the layout. Usually, when a layout is completed, it will stay that way through most of the game, so that if a column, pile, or row is removed, the space that is left can be filled with a card or a build.

rows, columns, and piles

In the layout, cards can be dealt into rows or columns. A **row** is a horizontal (dealt left to right) line of cards, and a **column** is a vertical (dealt top to bottom) line of cards. As you can see from the diagram below, columns are usually laid out so that each card peeks out a little bit from the one above it, so you can see all the cards in the column. Unless we say otherwise, columns should always be dealt this way. Rows, on the other hand, are often part of a layout and are usually dealt without overlapping.

Some games also have **piles** of cards, which just means that you deal a certain number of cards on top of one another. Like rows and columns, piles can be dealt face up or face down, but piles should be **squared up** so that you can't see any cards underneath the top card. Sometimes you will deal a single pile of cards called the **reserve**, which is different from other layout piles because you play the cards from a reserve pile, but never build on them.

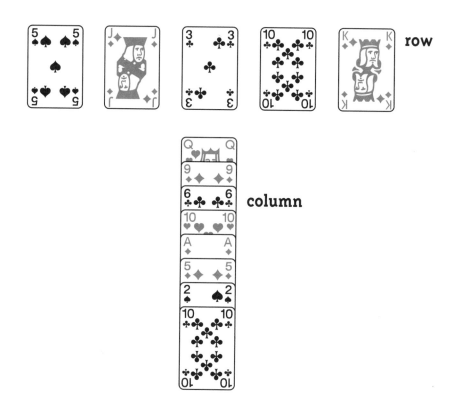

row

column

Because rows and columns are really just piles that have been spread out, only the top cards (those cards without any other cards on top of them) can be moved or played. All other cards beneath them, whether face up or face down, can be moved only when the cards on top have been removed. The exception to this is when you are moving a build (see page 7). Then, a sequence of cards is moved all at once, so that the top card is moved along with the cards beneath it.

stockpile and wastepile

Most solitaire games will have a layout with some cards left over. A face-down pile of these cards is called a **stockpile** or **stock**. During a game, turn these cards over according to the game's instructions and play them. When you have turned over a card but cannot play it, you'll most often put that card into another pile called the **wastepile**. Sometimes a game will allow you to redeal, and you'll use the wastepile again when there are no more cards left in the stockpile. When this happens, turn over the wastepile to make a new stockpile. A game will *not* allow you to redeal unless we tell you otherwise, so make sure you can't use a card before throwing it in the wastepile!

The object of almost every solitaire game is to complete all the **foundations**, piles of cards usually built up or down by suit. In a few games, you'll deal a card straight into the foundation at the start of the game, but most of the time, the foundations are piles of cards played just above or to the side of the rest of the layout, usually in a row. When you win your first solitaire game and see all your cards sitting in those neat foundations, you'll know why solitaire is worth all the work— and why it's so much fun!

SAMPLE LAYOUT
OF A GAME IN PROGRESS

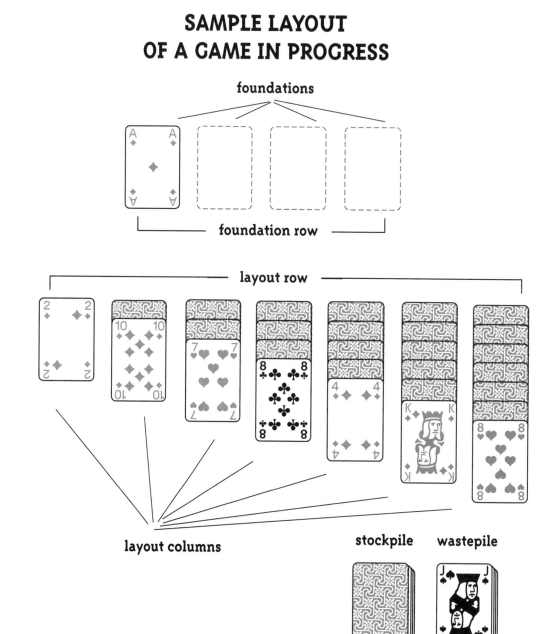

foundations

foundation row

layout row

layout columns

stockpile   wastepile

solitaire strategy

You will need to use different strategies in different games, but there are some good general rules to follow. First, realize that you don't always have to move a card to a foundation pile. Sometimes it's better to keep that card in your layout and build other cards on top of it. The only time you *must* move a card to a foundation is when it is the card that begins a foundation pile (usually an ace).

Solitaire requires planning and strategy. For most of the games, you'll need to stop and think every once in a while. For example, you might wonder, should I move this jack onto the foundation or keep it in the layout?

When games have rows or columns of face-up cards, so that you can see all or some of the cards underneath a top card, study all the cards to see which ones will help your game by continuing a build. Try to move the cards off the cards you can see you need. Plan ahead by looking for ways to move these cards.

When you have face-down piles in your layout, try and uncover them so that you can turn them over. Try to play the cards in your layout before the ones in your stockpile or wastepile, uncovering face-down cards whenever you can.

Sometimes when people play solitaire, they peek at the face-down cards. Some people call this cheating. Strictly speaking, you should turn over a face-down card only when it's available and then you should leave it turned over. But sometimes when you're learning, it's good to peek at some cards to get an idea of how one play will affect the game. You may even want to make several plays before replacing the cards the way they were, and then deciding. You be the judge of whether you will allow yourself to peek, remembering that you haven't *really* won a solitaire game unless you've done it without peeking.

In this book, specific strategies are outlined for almost every game. It's important to read the whole game's instructions and strategy completely before attempting to play a game for the first time.

how to use this book

We've organized these games beginning with the easiest and moving to the hardest. If you're new to solitaire, start with "Hit or Miss" and work your way forward. This way, you'll learn important basic solitaire strategy before moving to complicated games that build on these skills.

Remember that just because a game is easy to play, it doesn't mean it's easy to win! Many of the simplest games, like "Hit or Miss," "Double Jump," and "Pyramid," are easy to learn but incredibly hard to win. Other, more advanced games, like "Red and Black," "Precedence," and "Constitution," might take a little longer to learn, but you can win these often, after a little practice.

If you don't have a lot of room to play, such as if you're on a plane or in a car, stay with one-pack games like "Hit or Miss" that you can play without a table, or "Tower of Pisa," which takes only nine cards to play. Even "Contradance," a two-pack game, doesn't take that much room. When you've got room to spread out, try "Double Jump" or "Gaps," games where you have to lay out the whole deck, or two-pack games like "Grand Canyon" or "Sly Fox." You're sure to find lots of favorites here, because there are many games and variations to choose from!

Try These First

♠ ♥ ♣ ♦ ♠ ♥ ♣ ♦

Beginning Games

Hit or Miss

♠ ♥ ♣ ♦ ♠ ♥ ♣ ♦

Don't count this game out—or should you?

1. There is no layout for this game. Place the entire deck face down on the table to use as your stockpile.

2. Turn over the top card of the stock and say, "Ace."

3. If the top card *is* an ace, it is a "hit," so discard it. You will not use it again in the game. Otherwise, the card is a "miss," so place it face up in the wastepile.

4. Turn over the next card from the stock and say, "Two." Again, discard the card if it is a two (a hit) or put it in the wastepile if it is not (a miss).

5. Continue counting up, until you reach "King." Then start over again with "Ace." Discard any hits (cards with the same rank as the one you call out) and place the misses into the wastepile.

6. When you've used all the cards in the stockpile, turn over the wastepile without shuffling it. This is your new stock. Continue counting through the stock, discarding any hits.

7. You may continue to reuse the wastepile in this way, unless you count through the stock twice in a row without getting any hits. If this happens, the game is over.

8. If you hit all the cards in the deck, you win!

"Hit or Miss" can be played anywhere, even without a table. Just hold the cards in your hand as you count them out. Put your hits in your pocket or backpack. Return misses to the deck, face down at the bottom. If you have to stop before the game is over, wait until you get to "King." Put your discards face up on the bottom of the stock. When you want to play again, you can pick up where you left off by separating the discards back out, then counting the top card as "Ace."

Keep track of how many times you've gone through the stock by putting a piece of paper (or your finger) underneath the bottom card, then placing your discards below this. When the piece of paper works its way to the top of the stock, you've gone all the way through.

Tower of Pisa

♠ ♥ ♣ ♦ ♠ ♥ ♣ ♦

We're leaning toward calling this one our favorite

1. You need only nine cards for this game. Remove one each of the cards two through ten from a pack of cards. Suits don't matter.

2. Shuffle these cards, then deal them face up in three rows of three.

3. Only the cards at the bottom of the columns can be played, and they can only be played at the bottom of another column, below a card of higher rank.

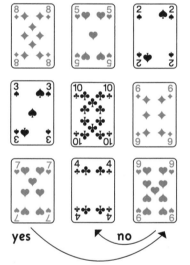

yes — no

4. If all the cards are removed from a column, either card from the bottom of the other two columns can be moved to begin a new one.

5. If you make a single column of all the cards, in descending order from ten to two, you win!

strategy: When filling an empty column, usually pick the higher of the two bottom cards. After you've played the game a few times, you will see how easy it is to move groups of cards one at a time from column to column, once those groups are in ranked order.

Doublet

♠ ♥ ♣ ♦ ♠ ♥ ♣ ♦

It's a-pair-ent how to win this game

1. Make a layout with twelve face-down piles of three cards each. Deal one more card face up on top of each pile. You should have four cards left over. Make a face-down pile of these for your stock.

2. Discard any pairs of face-up cards that are the same in suit *or* rank. Turn up the face-down cards underneath the pair you discard.

3. When a pile is completely discarded, turn over the top card of your stock and place it into the empty spot in the layout.

4. If you discard the entire deck—layout and stock—you win!

strategy: Pairs in suit are the most common, so try to discard pairs in rank first. Also, pay close attention late in the game to how many cards are left of the same suit or rank. Try to discard so that there's always an even number of these matching cards.

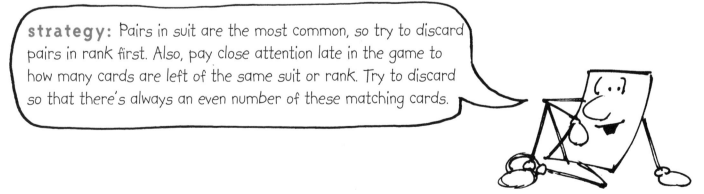

Double Jump

♠ ♥ ♣ ♦ ♠ ♥ ♣ ♦

Hop over all the cards to win

1. This game is best played on the floor, a large table, or anywhere else with lots of room. Deal all of your cards face up in a single row. The cards can overlap, but you might find it easier if they don't. If you have only a limited amount of room, you can also begin the game by dealing out just ten cards, adding more when you run out of moves or want to plan ahead.

2. When a card matches the card three cards to its right in rank or suit, "jump" the card on the left onto the card at right and square up the pile.

EXAMPLES OF POSSIBLE JUMPS

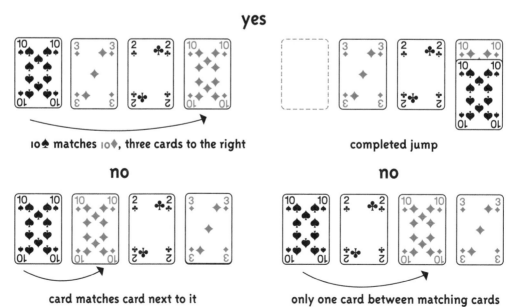

yes

10♠ matches 10♦, three cards to the right

completed jump

no

card matches card next to it

no

only one card between matching cards

3. Move the rest of the cards to the left to fill up the gaps left over after jumping cards. Doing this will open up other jumps. Piles of cards are moved or jumped over all together, as if they are only one card, using just the rank and color of the top card.

4. Continue jumping cards in this way, until no more jumps can be made. You win if the whole deck is reduced to just three piles.

strategy: This game requires advance planning. Look ahead to see how jumping (and therefore removing) a card will open up other jumps. Pay attention to the top cards, noticing how changing the order of jumps will change the top card on a pile.

variation: **Accordion** is a tougher version of this game. You can jump a card onto another card either three cards away (as in "Double Jump") or onto the card next to it. But to win at "Accordion," you need to reduce the whole deck to just one pile, something that's almost impossible to do. Consider yourself a winner if you end up with five piles or fewer.

Auld Lang Syne

♠ ♥ ♣ ♦ ♠ ♥ ♣ ♦

The solitaire game everyone sings about on New Year's Eve

1. Remove the four aces from the deck and place them face up in a row that doesn't overlap. These will be the beginnings of your foundations, and you'll build up on them by suit.

2. Deal four cards face up in a row underneath the foundations. This is your layout.

3. Play whichever cards you can from the layout onto the foundations. There is no building in the layout.

4. When you've played all the cards you can, deal another row of face-up cards on top of the layout row. Do not play any cards until all four new cards have been dealt out. Then continue playing any cards that you can from the top of each pile.

5. Cards in the layout piles may be played when they are uncovered. If you play all of the cards in a layout pile, you may *not* move any cards to the space. Simply fill the space with a card the next time you deal out four cards.

6. It's very difficult to move all the cards to the foundations. But if you do, you win!

> **strategy:** There isn't much strategy to this game, because it depends completely on how the cards turn up in the layout piles. Just make sure you've played all the cards you can *before* dealing out another row of four.

variation: Tam O'Shanter is even harder to win. Don't pull the aces out of the deck at the beginning, but play them to the foundations as they appear in the layout piles. If you can win "Tam O' Shanter," you're a real solitaire champ!

Triplets

Can you handle three at a time?

1. Deal the cards into eighteen piles—sixteen piles of three cards each, then into two piles of two cards each. Turn over the top cards on all the piles. This is your layout, and there is no stock.

2. Look for three cards with consecutive ranks, without paying attention to their suits. In other words, make triplets by matching a card with the card one rank below it and the card one rank above it—7-8-9, 3-4-5, or J-Q-K, for example. Cards from any one of the eighteen piles can be used together to create triplets.

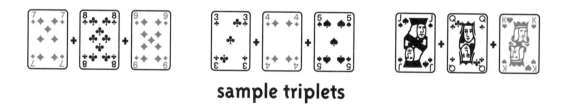

sample triplets

3. Kings can be either high or low in this game, but not both. Aces are always low. So a king may be used in a J-Q-K triplet, or in a K-A-2 triplet, but not in a Q-K-A triplet.

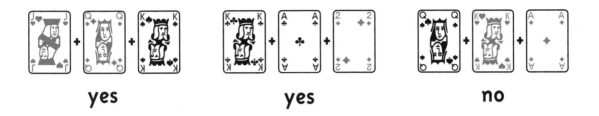

yes   **yes**   **no**

4. Whenever a card is removed from a pile, turn over the card on top of that pile. Empty piles cannot be filled.

5. Try to remove fifty-one cards in sets of three like this, leaving one card. If you can, you're a winner!

strategy: If you have to decide between two cards to make up a set, use the one with more cards below it in the pile. Removing all the cards in a pile, usually a good solitaire strategy, doesn't help you in this game.

Lucky Thirteen

Thirteen could be your lucky number!

1. Deal the cards into thirteen face-down piles of four cards each and turn over the top card of each pile. This is the layout for the game, and there is no stock.

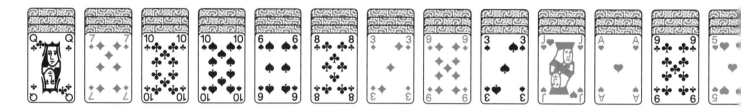

2. Build down on each pile, paying no attention to suit. When a face-down card is exposed, turn it over.

3. You may only move the top card from each pile. No full or partial builds may be moved.

4. As you find the aces, put them above the layout to begin the foundations. The foundations build up in suit, from ace to king.

5. When you remove all the cards from a pile, you may move any available card to the space this creates in the layout.

GAME IN PROGRESS

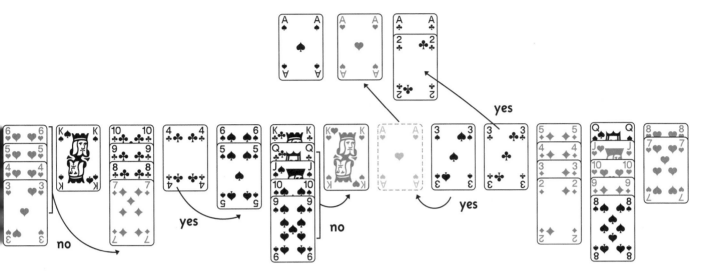

6. Move all the cards to the foundations to be a winner!

strategy: Build in suit on the layout whenever possible, and start building with the highest cards. Try not to make long builds at the beginning of the game, since they can be difficult to remove.

Look for moves that you can undo easily. If there are two sixes exposed, don't hesitate to play a five on either one of them, because it can always be moved to the other six.

Also, work to remove all the cards in a pile, so you can move a high card to the space.

It Follows

♠ ♥ ♣ ♦ ♠ ♥ ♣ ♦

The only suit that doesn't matter is your birthday suit

1. Deal a layout of six face-up cards in a row. The four foundations will be placed above this row. All the other cards will be your stock.

2. For this game, you must use the following order of suits when building on your layout: clubs, diamonds, spades, and hearts, then back to clubs again. So a diamond can be played only on a club, and a spade only on a diamond, and a heart only on a spade. Clubs are then played on hearts, and the order continues. Pay close attention to this when you are playing, because breaking this order makes winning the game impossible.

order:

3. Cards should be played in your layout in this suit order, without paying any attention to rank. Build in each layout column, filling any open spaces that you create in the layout from the top card in your stock or from the wastepile. Builds cannot be moved into empty layout spaces.

4. You can move full or partial builds.

5. When an ace is revealed, it will start one of the foundation piles. The foundations also follow the order of suits, so that the first (far left) foundation pile begins with the ace of clubs, the second foundation begins with the ace of diamonds, and so forth.

6. Build up on the foundations according to this order. Only a two of diamonds can be built up on the ace of clubs, and only a three of spades can be built on this two of diamonds. Again, if you don't follow this order, you can't win the game.

7. When no more moves can be made from the layout, turn over the top card of your stock and try to play it. If you can't, move it—face up—to the wastepile. The top card of the wastepile is always available for play.

GAME IN PROGRESS

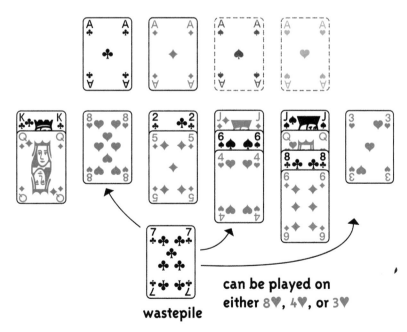

wastepile

can be played on
either 8♥, 4♥, or 3♥

8. Continue turning over cards from your stock when you can't play from the layout or wastepile. The game is over when you've turned over the whole stockpile and can't play any more cards.

9. You win the game if all the foundations are built up to kings.

strategy: When you're building on your layout, try to keep the lowest cards at the bottom of the columns. This will make them more accessible, since you'll need to use them on the foundations sooner than high cards.

Also, learn to move builds around the layout so that you can expose cards you need to play. If you need the four of hearts, but there are cards on top of it, look for another heart at the bottom of a column in the layout. If you find one, play the build covering the four of hearts on this heart. Now you can use the four of hearts!

Try to have all your cards in as many columns as possible, especially late in the game. Don't build everything into one or two columns, or you'll have no place to play.

Learning
Solitaire
Skills

♠♥♣♦♠♥♣♦

Easy
Games

Puss in Corner

One card goes kitty-corner to another

1. Pull the four aces out of the deck and put them in a square. These will be the foundations. Deal one card from the pack at the corner of each ace to create the layout.

2. Build up the foundations by the same color (black on black and red on red), from ace to king. You may play only the top card from any of the four layout piles onto the foundations.

3. When you cannot play any more cards, deal four more cards to the layout piles, then try and play those cards. You may choose which card to place on which pile, rather than just dealing the cards out in order, and this is part of the strategy in this game. But do not play any cards until all four have been dealt out.

4. You may redeal the cards once, after you've gone through the stock. Gather the layout cards, keeping them in their piles, and turn them over. Do not shuffle the cards. Deal four more cards and begin again.

5. If you move all the cards to the foundations, you win!

strategy: When dealing and placing cards, try to place them on higher cards. This makes them easier to move. If you can avoid it, don't play a card on another card of the same rank.

variation: Old Patience is a more difficult (and more popular) version of this game. In "Old Patience," do not pull out the aces at the beginning, but move them to the foundations as they become available in the layout. Build up the foundations from ace to king, ignoring both color and suit. There is no redeal in this game.

Captive Queens

♠ ♥ ♣ ♦ ♠ ♥ ♣ ♦

The queens never get out of this game

1. The layout for this game will be built as you play. At the beginning, all you need is a shuffled deck of cards. The game is played simply by turning over the cards in the deck one at a time.

2. "Captive Queens" has eight foundations, building on the fives and sixes in the deck. As you turn over a five or a six, place it as shown in the diagram.

3. The queens aren't used, except as decoration. As you turn a queen over, put it in the middle of your layout, as shown.

4. Build up in suit on the sixes, until you reach jacks. Build down in suit on the fives, to kings. Kings are played on aces in this game.

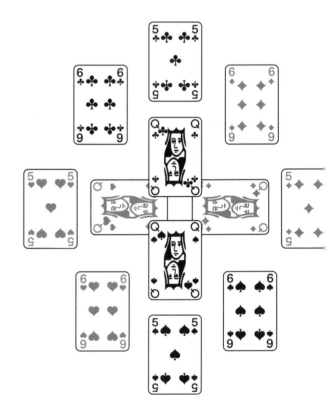

5. When you have gone all the way through the deck once, you should have all your foundations and queens in place and probably some cards played on those foundations.

6. Cards that cannot be played are placed in a wastepile. You can redeal twice by turning over the wastepile and continuing to draw from the top.

7. If you play the whole deck onto the layout, so that all you can see are kings, queens (in the middle), and jacks—you win!

strategy: Make sure you can't play a card before discarding it, especially the first time through the deck, where it's sometimes easy to miss a foundation card.

King's Audience

♠ ♥ ♣ ♦ ♠ ♥ ♣ ♦

Can you get all the cards in to see the king?

1. Deal sixteen cards in a square, four cards on each side, to make your layout. These cards create the antechamber, which was the room where people waited to see the king. You want to get all the cards inside the antechamber for an audience with the king.

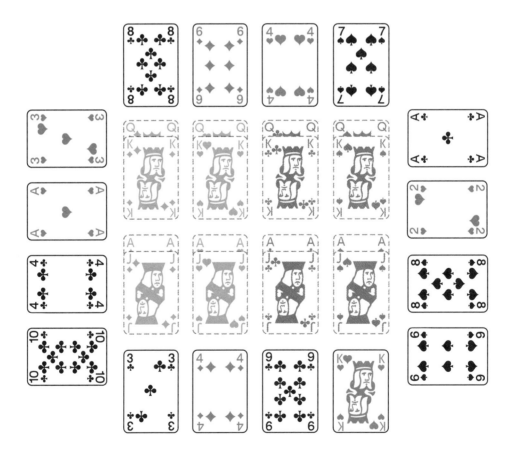

2. The foundations are the jacks, but they can only be placed inside the antechamber with the ace of the same suit. When you have both, put the jack inside the antechamber with the ace underneath. You may cover the ace completely; once you place it under the jack, you will not use the ace again.

3. When you have a king and queen of the same suit, put them inside the antechamber, above the foundations. Once they have reached this point, the kings and queens will not be used again.

4. Turn over cards one at a time from the stock and build down in suit on the foundations to the two. If a card cannot be used, discard it face up in a pile. You may use only the top card of this wastepile.

5. You may also play any card from the layout to the foundations. Fill any space with the top card from the wastepile or from your stock. (No peeking!) If you build down to two on all foundations, you've gotten an audience with the king—and you win!

strategy: Pay attention to the aces and face cards as you turn them over. They will usually be played somewhere, since they are either played before, or separately from, the other cards.

Whenever possible, fill spaces in the antechamber with cards from the wastepile, since you will be able to play the top card in your stock anyway.

Westcliff

♠ ♥ ♣ ♦ ♠ ♥ ♣ ♦

This card game leaves you hanging around

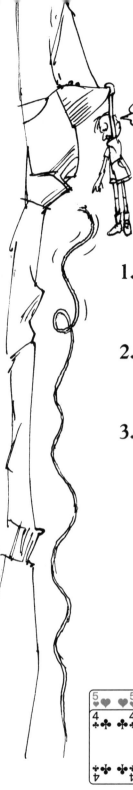

1. Deal thirty cards into ten face-down piles of three cards each. Turn over the top card of each pile.

2. The foundations will begin with the aces, when they are turned over, and you will build up in suit on these aces.

3. The layout piles build down in alternating colors, on the top card of any pile or build. When a face-down card is exposed, turn it over. If you create an empty space in the layout, you can fill it with any available card or build.

GAME IN PROGRESS

4. You may move single cards or completed builds from the tops of your layout piles, but not partial builds, not even the top card of any build. In other words, any time you play cards from one layout pile to another, you must expose a face-down card.

5. When you cannot play any more layout cards, begin turning over the cards in your stock one at a time. If a stock card cannot be played, put it face up in the wastepile. The top card of the wastepile is available to be played anytime.

6. If you move the whole deck to the foundations, you win!

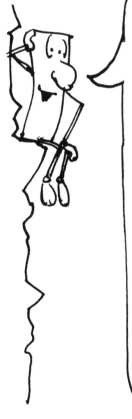

strategy: Building is at the heart of this game, but be careful not to make builds that are too long, since this may bury important cards under other cards. Build only when doing so would expose a face-down card or create a space to play another card or build. Building just for the sake of building can get you into trouble.

When deciding between playing two cards from your layout, try to eliminate a pile of face-down cards to create a space. This gives you flexibility, since it can be filled with any available card or build from the layout, stock, or wastepile.

This is an easier version of "Canfield" and "Klondike," two of the most popular forms of solitaire. Play this game as a warm-up before tackling these tougher games, which use many of the same strategies you'll learn here.

For an easier game of "Westcliff," allow yourself to move partial builds around the layout.

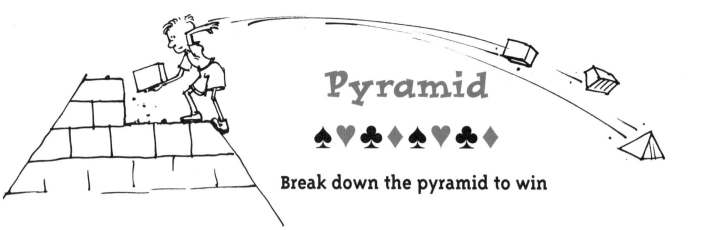

Pyramid

♠ ♥ ♣ ♦ ♠ ♥ ♣ ♦

Break down the pyramid to win

1. Deal twenty-eight cards into the pyramid layout shown below, with the last row containing seven cards. Notice how each row is overlapped by the row beneath it, and each card is overlapped by two cards.

2. Only those cards without any cards overlapping them are available. All other cards can be played only when you remove the two cards directly below them in the pyramid. So, at the beginning of the game, only the seven cards in the bottom row of the layout can be removed.

3. Cards are valued for this game according to their rank—kings are worth thirteen points, queens are worth twelve, jacks are worth eleven, and so on, down to the ace, which is worth one. The number cards are all worth the same value as the number on them.

4. Any two available cards whose value adds up to thirteen may be removed and discarded, as below. For example, a seven and a six may be removed, or a two and a jack. Kings are removed by themselves when they become available.

5. Remove any cards you can from the layout, then begin turning over cards one at a time from the stock. Unusable cards are placed face up in a wastepile, and the top card of this pile is available.

GAME IN PROGRESS

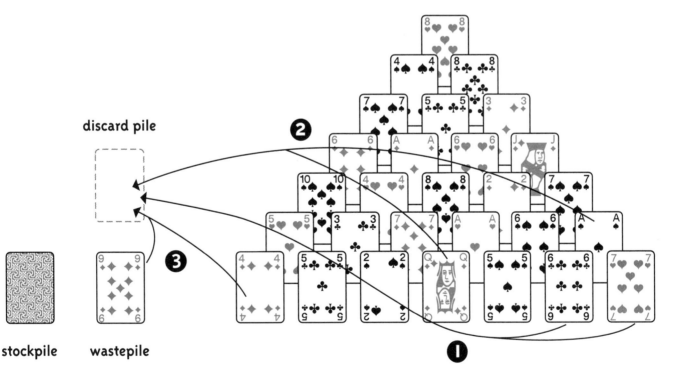

discard pile

stockpile   wastepile

6. Available cards in the stock or wastepile may be played with cards in the layout or with one another (i.e., you can play the stock card with the top card of the wastepile).

7. When you have played all the cards in the stock, turn over the wastepile and continue playing. You may redeal like this twice.

8. If you remove all the cards from the layout and the stock, you win!

strategy: Whenever you're faced with a decision about which cards to remove, first remove cards from the layout, especially when a card is covering more than one card.

variation: Place all cards removed from the layout in a separate pile, face up. Any available card not in the layout may be paired with the top card of this pile of removed cards and also removed—the removed card can be removed again.

Par Pyramid: Because it is a hard game to win, players have developed a scoring system for "Pyramid." Play against yourself or one or more friends. Each person plays six games of "Pyramid" and adds up his or her score according to these rules:

Winning the game: Fifty points for eliminating all cards in the layout and stock.

Removing the pyramid on the first deal: If you remove all the cards from the pyramid without redealing, continue to play out the cards in your stock against the top card in the wastepile, discarding consecutive pairs totalling thirteen. You may redeal twice. You get fifty points, minus the value of whatever cards are left after all the redeals.

Removing the pyramid on the second deal: This is worth thirty-five points, minus the value of your remaining cards. You may not redeal.

Removing the pyramid on the third deal: This is worth twenty points, minus the value of your remaining cards. You may not redeal.

Not removing the pyramid at all: If, after your two redeals, there are still some cards in the layout, you get no points. Subtract the value of all remaining cards (layout cards plus cards in the wastepile) from your score, using negative numbers when necessary. It is possible after one or more games of "Par Pyramid" to end up with a negative score. If you're playing alone, *any positive score* means you've won. That should show you how difficult "Par Pyramid" can be!

Grandfather's Clock

♠ ♥ ♣ ♦ ♠ ♥ ♣ ♦

A granddaddy of a clock game

1. Remove the following cards from the deck: two of hearts, three of spades, four of diamonds, five of clubs, six of hearts, seven of spades, eight of diamonds, nine of clubs, ten of hearts, jack of spades, queen of diamonds, king of clubs. These will begin your foundations, which are arranged like the numbers on a clock.

2. Place the two of hearts at the five o'clock position, then place the other ones, in order, around the clock face, as shown. Shuffle and deal the rest of the cards into eight face-up columns of five cards each.

3. Build up the foundations in suit until they reach the number representing their position on the clock. For example, the two of hearts will be built up to the five of hearts, since it is in the five o'clock position. Jacks represent elevens, and end building at the eleven o'clock spot; queens represent twelves and are used for twelve o'clock. No foundation will end with a king, but aces are played on kings in foundations.

4. Only cards at the bottom of the layout columns may be played. These cards may be played on the foundations or can be built down on other layout columns, paying no attention to suit or color.

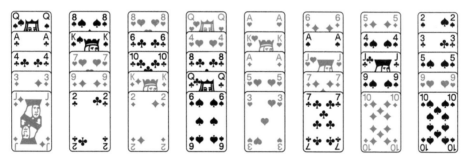

5. If you remove all the cards in a layout column, you may move any one available card to the space this creates. You may not move more than one card at a time. No full or partial builds may be moved.

6. If you move all the cards to the clock face, you win!

strategy: Don't build too many cards on one layout column, since they can be hard to remove. Look for the cards you need in the layout, and try to move the cards covering those cards.

Flower Garden

♠ ♥ ♣ ♦ ♠ ♥ ♣ ♦

What grows when you plant a deck of cards?
Queen Anne's Lace? Jackfruit?

1. Deal a layout with six columns of six face-up cards. This is your garden. Spread all the other cards below the garden in a curved row, called the bouquet.

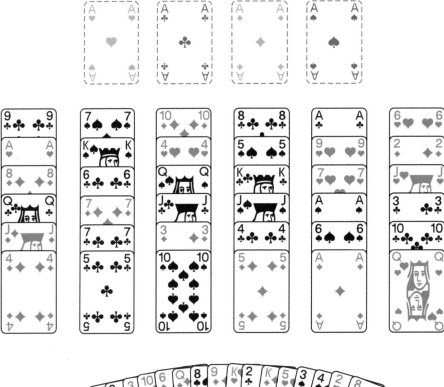

2. The four aces begin the foundations, which are played above the garden. Move the aces as they become available and build up on them in suit to kings.

3. All the cards in the bouquet can be played, as can the cards at the bottom of the columns in the garden. Build down on the garden, paying no attention to color or suit.

4. Only one card may be moved at a time from one column to another. No full or partial builds may be moved.

5. If you remove all the cards from a column in the garden, fill the space with any card that can be played.

6. If you move all the cards to the foundations, you win the game!

strategy: Don't play from the bouquet onto the garden, unless you can't play any other card or if doing so will allow you to move a lot of other cards. Once you move a card to the garden and start putting other cards on top of it, the card becomes very difficult to play. Leaving it in the bouquet will make it available at any time. Don't build long columns, especially on top of low cards, as it will be very hard for you to remove all the cards.

Gaps

♠ ♥ ♣ ♦ ♠ ♥ ♣ ♦

A game of fill-in-the-blanks

1. For the layout in this game, deal the entire deck into four rows of thirteen face-up cards, one row just above the other. These rows will be both the foundations and the layout. Remove all the aces from the layout, as shown below, but do not move the layout to fill in the four spaces, or gaps, that this creates.

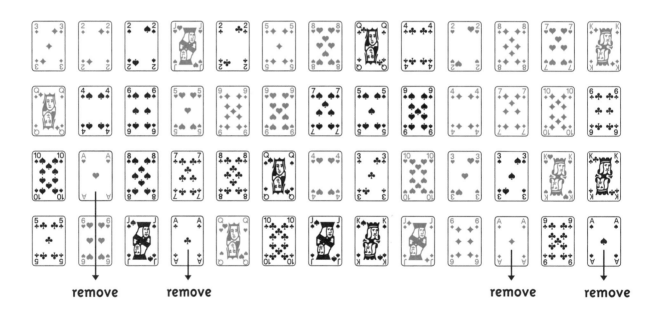

remove   remove   remove   remove

2. In "Gaps," you build up in suit by moving cards into these four spaces, so that there is only one card in the deck that can be moved into any particular gap.

3. Look at the card just to the left of any of the four gaps and find the card in the layout that is the same suit and is one rank higher than this card. Move the card you've found to this space. You should now have two consecutive cards of the same suit right next to each other with the lower card on the left. For example, if a jack of spades has a gap to the right of it, that gap can be filled only with the queen of spades.

move Q♠ to the gap

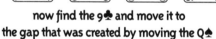

now find the 9♣ and move it to the gap that was created by moving the Q♠

4. Now you can play into the gap you created by moving a card.

5. Gaps to the right of a king cannot be filled and are blocked, but these gaps can be moved by moving the king next to them. You may have two or more gaps in a row after several moves are made.

6. Gaps at the far left of any row in the layout are filled with any two. Once a two has begun a row, that two, along with all cards you move to the right of it, is locked. Locked cards are not moved again, not even in a redeal.

7. Whenever play is blocked (all four gaps appear to the right of a king), collect all the cards in the layout *except* any locked cards. Leave the locked cards just as they are in the layout.

8. Shuffle these remaining cards. Leaving a gap to the right of each row of locked cards, deal the cards and continue playing. If a row does not have any locked cards in it, leave a gap at the far left of the row, so that you can play a two there. You may redeal in this way twice.

9. The object of the game is to get the entire deck lined up in order, by suit, in the four rows. If you can do this—and it's very difficult— you win!

strategy: Rather than moving cards willy-nilly, plan your moves in advance so that you (1) open a gap at the left of a row, (2) open a gap to the right of a locked card, or (3) move a King away from a gap, so that your move is not blocked.

variation: For an even more difficult version, shuffle the aces back into the deck each time you redeal. Do not leave any gaps in your layout when you deal these cards back out, but remove the aces, as in step 1. Continue play in the gaps that this creates.

Easy
as
1-2-3

♠♥♣♠♦♠♥♣♦

Counting
Games

Eleven

Get those elevens out of here!

1. Deal a layout of nine face-up cards, in three rows of three cards each. The rest of the deck is your stockpile.

2. Discard all pairs that total eleven, counting aces as one and all other cards as their face values.

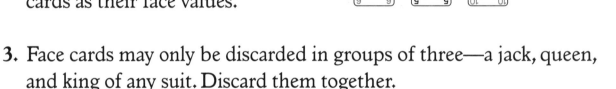

discard pile

3. Face cards may only be discarded in groups of three—a jack, queen, and king of any suit. Discard them together.

4. Deal from your stockpile to fill spaces created by discards.

5. The game is over when no more cards can be removed from your layout. If you discard the entire deck before this happens, you win!

strategy: Know your addition! Pairs that add up to eleven are: one and ten, two and nine, three and eight, four and seven, five and six.

Block Eleven

Block all twelve piles with elevens

1. Deal twelve face-up cards, in three rows of four cards each. These cards will begin the layout piles.

2. If any face cards are showing, place them at the bottom of the deck. Replace them with cards from the top of the deck. Continue to do this until there are no face cards showing. The remainder of the deck, including the face cards at the bottom, will be your stockpile.

3. If no face cards show after the first deal, make sure to put the first face card that turns up during play at the bottom of the deck, and replace it with another card. You can't win this game unless the last card in the deck is a face card!

4. When you find a pair of cards in the layout that adds up to eleven, deal one card from your stock face up on each card in the pair. Count aces as one and all other cards as their rank values. When a face card is dealt on a pile, that pile can no longer be used, unless it is the first face card dealt in step 3.

5. The game ends when no more cards remain in the stockpile, or if no moves remain. If all twelve piles are covered with face cards, you win!

Thirteens

♠ ♥ ♣ ♦ ♠ ♥ ♣ ♦

Make your pairs fall out right to win

1. Deal fifteen cards face up into three columns that don't overlap. Put the rest of the deck next to this layout, to be used as your stockpile.

2. Look for pairs of cards that total thirteen. These pairs must be next to each other, either vertically, horizontally, or diagonally.

3. Count aces as one, jacks as eleven, queens as twelve, and kings as thirteen. Remove kings singly (in other words, without having to make a pair).

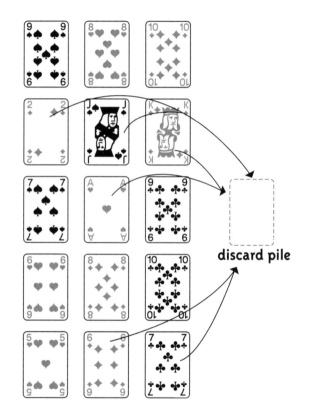

4. When you have found a pair, remove it. After each removal, fill in the spaces by moving an entire column down, as though the cards are falling into place (see diagram, following page). Add new cards from the stock at the top of the columns.

5. When an entire column has been removed, you may move the top card from another column to the bottom of the empty column.

6. If you remove the entire deck, you win!

strategy: Pay attention to how each move affects other moves, either *blocking* or creating pairs. Sometimes moves need to be made in a particular order so that you can remove as many cards as possible. Plan ahead.

EXAMPLE OF HOW CARDS "FALL" INTO PLACE

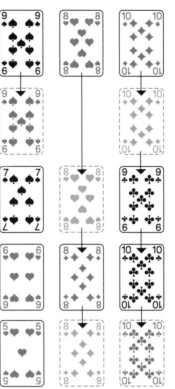

fourteen Out

♠ ♥ ♣ ♦ ♠ ♥ ♣ ♦

Are you out of fourteens yet?

1. Deal the whole deck into twelve face-up columns so you can see all the cards. There will be five cards in the first four columns, and four in every other one.

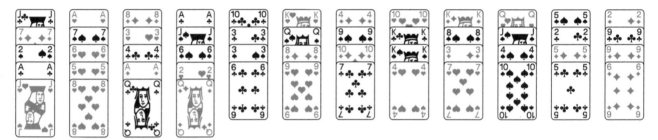

2. Only cards on top of columns can be played. Discard any two cards that add up to fourteen. Aces count as one, jacks as eleven, queens as twelve, and kings as thirteen. When a column is completely discarded, the space left behind cannot be filled.

3. If you discard the whole deck, you're a winner!

strategy: Don't leave important cards at the bottoms of piles. If you need to remove nines from the tops of piles, for example, try to uncover the fives. Also, be careful not to block yourself. For example, imagine having one pile with a ten on top and a three somewhere underneath it, and another pile with a jack on top and a four underneath it. Use another four to match with the ten or another three to match with the jack, or you'll be stuck.

Fifteen

How many ways can you add up to fifteen?

1. Deal sixteen cards in four face-up rows of four cards each. The rest of the deck is your stockpile.

2. Discard sets of cards that add up to fifteen, counting aces as one and all other cards as their rank values. Sets of cards can be three, four, or as many as it takes.

3. Discard face cards with tens, in groups of four —a jack, queen, king, and ten. These cards can be of any suit.

4. Fill any spaces in the layout from your stockpile.

5. If you discard all the cards in the deck, you win!

strategy: Discard cards in groups as large as possible, especially early on. Pay attention to the way lower ranked cards can add up to high numbers. Instead of discarding a seven and an eight, for example, discard a seven, a five, a two, and a one. This will give you more cards to choose from, which is important when you're trying to get rid of face cards.

Double Your Fun

Twice as good as your average game!

1. Deal eight cards into two columns of three, with a column of two in the middle, as shown. The bottom card in the middle column will be the foundation pile, which is built upon as described below.

foundation pile

2. If any kings appear anywhere in the layout, place them at the bottom of the deck and replace them with another card. Once the layout is free of kings, the rest of the deck is your stockpile.

3. There is no building on the layout, only on the foundation. The card that can be played on the foundation is determined by doubling the value of the card that is already there. When this total is fourteen or more, you must subtract thirteen to figure out the correct value. Kings have no value. See the conversion chart on the following page to check your math.

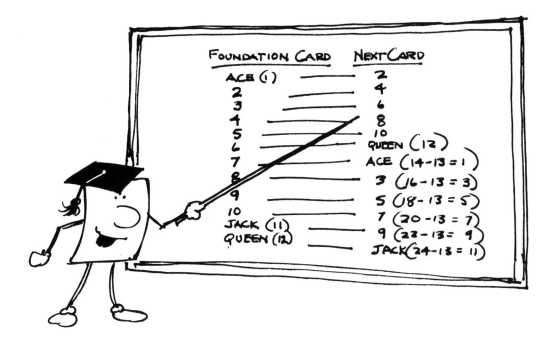

FOUNDATION CARD   NEXT CARD

ACE (1) ————————— 2
2 ——————————————— 4
3 ——————————————— 6
4 ——————————————— 8
5 ——————————————— 10
6 ——————————————— QUEEN (12)
7 ——————————————— ACE (14 - 13 = 1)
8 ——————————————— 3 (16 - 13 = 3)
9 ——————————————— 5 (18 - 13 = 5)
10 —————————————— 7 (20 - 13 = 7)
JACK (11) ———————— 9 (22 - 13 = 9)
QUEEN (12) ———————— JACK (24 - 13 = 11)

4. Remember that kings have no value, so do not appear on the chart. When a king appears on a layout pile, that pile is blocked and may not be used again for the rest of the game.

5. Play whatever cards you can from the seven layout cards onto the foundation. Replace these cards from your stockpile or wastepile, whichever you choose. If you choose to fill a space from the wastepile, you must use whatever card you turn over (rather than turning over cards until you find one you like).

6. Once you cannot play any cards from the layout, turn over cards in your stockpile one at a time. Discard unplayable cards face up to a single wastepile. The top card of this wastepile is always available to play to the layout or to the foundation.

7. When you have gone through all the cards in the stockpile, redeal by turning over the wastepile to make a new stockpile. You may do this twice.

8. If you move all the cards except the kings to the foundation, you double your fun and win!

strategy: Kings are the most important cards to avoid here, so don't put them on the layout unless you are forced to. Later in the game, however, you may have to play a King into the layout in order to get to a card in the wastepile. Just hope that this doesn't happen too often.

10-20-30

♠ ♥ ♣ ♦ ♠ ♥ ♣ ♦

A perfect ten—and more!

1. There is no layout for this game, although it may take up lots of space. To play, deal cards one at a time from the deck into a row.

2. Discard any adjacent (next to each other in the row) cards that add up to ten, twenty, or thirty. Count aces as one, other cards as their rank values, and all face cards as ten.

3. You may discard only in sets of two or more and they must be adjacent. When you remove cards, move the row together to close up the space.

4. You are not required to discard a set of cards immediately. Sometimes it's better to wait for the next card, which may allow you to discard more cards (for example, if your total is ten, and the next card is a face card). If you have the space and the patience, you can deal the entire deck in a row before discarding a single card!

5. If you can discard the entire deck, you score a perfect ten!

Calculation

♠ ♥ ♣ ♦ ♠ ♥ ♣ ♦

A game to test your card and math skills to the limit

1. Take any ace, two, three, and four from the deck. Place them side-by-side and in this order to begin your four foundations. You will build four layout piles (they are actually wastepiles) below these foundations as you play. The rest of the cards are your stockpile.

2. The foundations are built up—without paying attention to suit—in four different ways, depending on the bottom card:

Build the first foundation by ones—A, 2, 3, 4, etc., all the way to K
Build the second foundation by twos—2, 4, 6, 8, 10, Q, A, 3, 5, 7, 9, J, K
Build the third foundation by threes—3, 6, 9, Q, 2, 5, 8, J, A, 4, 7, 10, K
Build the fourth foundation by fours—4, 8, Q, 3, 7, J, 2, 6, 10, A, 5, 9, K

3. Notice that each foundation begins with the value that it increases by. Count aces as one, jacks as eleven, queens as twelve, and use kings to finish each foundation (they have no value). When you reach a total over thirteen, just subtract thirteen to find the next card that belongs on that foundation.

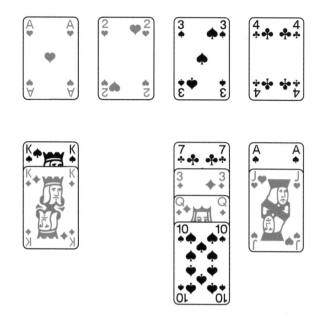

4. Turn cards over from your stockpile one at a time. If you cannot play a card to a foundation, place it in one of the four layout piles.

5. Continue going through the deck, discarding unplayable cards. The top card of each layout pile can be played at any time on the foundations, but otherwise the layout cards cannot be moved.

6. You may choose which layout pile to discard to each time, and the order of the cards in these piles can be very important. You may spread out the cards in the layout piles if you want to, so you can keep track of all the cards in a pile.

7. Spaces made by removing all the cards in a layout pile are filled from the stockpile, not from the layout piles.

8. You are allowed two redeals. Collect the cards in the layout piles into a new stockpile and start going through them one at a time again.

9. If you move all the cards to the foundations, you're a winner!

strategy: The order of the cards in each layout pile is extremely important, as are the cards in the piles. Build cards in the layout piles according to one of the foundation rules whenever possible, so you can move them, one after another, to a foundation pile. Remember, however, that these sequences will have to be built in reverse on a layout pile in order to move the cards to the foundation.

Try and hold one pile for Kings only, since it will be hard to remove these until late in the game. Try not to place two cards of the same rank on top of each other, as these will also be difficult to remove.

A
Real
Challenge

♠♥♣♦♠♥♣♦

Advanced
Games

Battle of the Ladies

Which queen will win the jack?

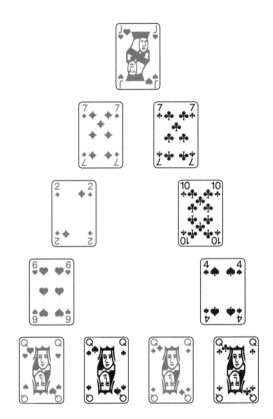

1. Remove all the queens and the jacks from the deck. Put the queens in a row at the bottom of your layout. They will begin the foundations, which are built up in suit, playing an ace on a king, and a two on an ace. Discard three of the jacks and place the fourth (of any suit) a good distance above the foundation row. The queens will be battling to see who wins this jack.

2. Deal six cards to form a pyramid, stretching three on a side downward from the jack to the queens. Leave plenty of room between the layout piles so you may build on them in rows. This completes your layout, and the rest of your cards are placed face down in a stockpile below the layout.

3. Layout cards may be played onto the foundations, or built down in alternating colors on each other. You may only move single cards, not full or partial builds.

4. When you remove all the cards in a layout row, fill the space with the top card from your stockpile.

5. Once you have made all the moves you can, deal six more cards on top of all the layout piles. Do not make any moves until all six cards have been dealt. Then continue playing, building on the top card of the layout pile, regardless of whether it continues a build below that card.

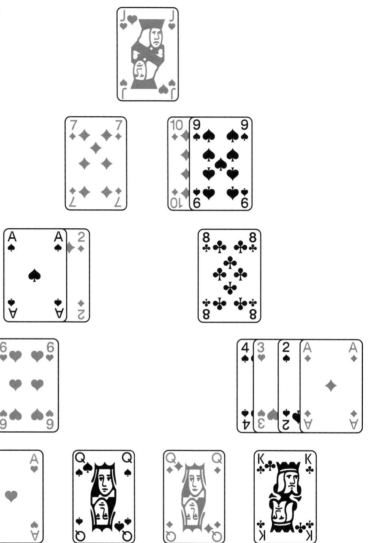

GAME IN PROGRESS

6. Many times, you will not have enough cards to complete the final six-card deal. Just deal as many cards as you have, beginning with the bottom left pile and proceeding clockwise. Play when you are finished dealing.

7. If you have not finished by the time you've dealt all the cards from the stockpile, you may redeal twice. Keeping the cards in order, collect the pile on the bottom left of the layout, turn it over, then place the pile on the bottom right on top of it, face down. Then collect the pile at the middle left, then middle right, and so on until the whole layout is picked up. Do not shuffle. Redeal the layout as in step 2 and continue playing.

8. The first queen to complete her foundation pile (a ten will be the top card when this happens) wins the jack and the game is over.

strategy : It's tempting in this game to pick a favorite suit early on and then build only on that foundation. But you'll need to build evenly, at least at the beginning of the game. Toward the end of the game, you will often be faced with a choice of which suit to finish. Play several games until you can win each suit!

variation: If you prefer to have the jacks chase the queen, you may place a queen at the top and begin the foundation rows with jacks. Build downward in suit on the jacks until you reach kings (which are played on the aces).

Fortune Teller uses the same rules and layout as "Battle of the Ladies," but you can use it to tell your fortune. Write down four fortunes for yourself, or have a friend write some down for you. Mix them together and randomly put one under each queen. Play the game until one queen wins, redealing as many times as necessary. Read the fortune under that queen to find out your future! As a fun party game, make a bunch of fortunes and have each person pick four and play "Fortune Teller."

Weddings

♠ ♥ ♣ ♦ ♠ ♥ ♣ ♦

Get the cards all paired off in this romantic game

1. Deal five columns of four cards each as shown in below left diagram.

2. In this game, you can remove any cards of the same rank that are next to each other—vertically, horizontally, or diagonally. Once a pair is removed, you cannot remove new pairs with a space between them.

3. After you remove all the possible pairs, fill the spaces with the other cards in the layout. Starting with the highest row, move cards to the

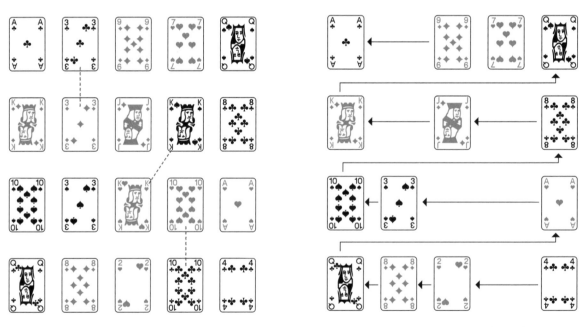

find and remove pairs that "touch"   **then move cards to the left to fill spaces**

left to fill any spaces. Fill gaps in the extreme right side of a row by moving up the card, or cards, at the extreme left of the row beneath it.

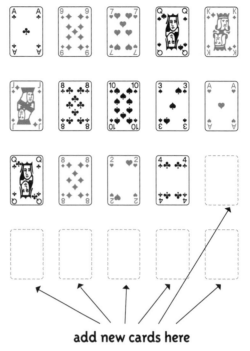

add new cards here

4. After you have finished, you should have an even number of spaces in the bottom row or rows. Deal cards from the stockpile to fill these spaces and then remove pairs again.

5. Continue removing pairs and adjusting the layout. If you can remove the whole deck, you win!

strategy: This game requires planning only when you have a choice of pairs to remove among three of the same card. Look at how removing different pairs will affect other pairs when you rearrange the layout. Remove the pair that gives you the most possible moves when the layout is rearranged and redealt. If neither play seems to give you any advantage, remove cards from higher rows first.

variation: Try using smaller layouts for a harder game, or larger layouts for an easier version.

Castles in Spain

♠ ♥ ♣ ♦ ♠ ♥ ♣ ♦

In this game, Spanish castles look like pyramids

1. The layout in this game is thirteen piles dealt into a pyramid, with five piles on the bottom row, four piles above that, then three piles, and one pile on top. Each pile has three face-down cards and one face-up card on top. You should have no cards left over after dealing the layout. Square up the piles after you deal.

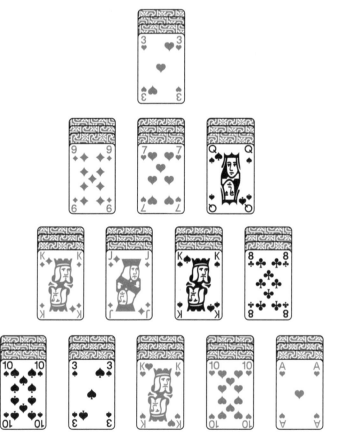

2. The foundations will begin with aces, placed above the layout as they turn up. Build up the foundations by suit.

3. Build down in the layout in alternating colors, moving single cards, partial builds, or full builds.

4. Turn over face-down cards when you move the cards off them.

5. Move any card, full build, or partial build to a space when an entire pile is removed from the layout. You must fill a space immediately before continuing play.

6. Move all the cards from the layout to the foundations, and you've conquered a Spanish castle!

strategy: Try to move cards to create spaces or to expose the face-down cards. Build on the foundations when you can, but don't build too high too quickly. Aces must be moved to the foundations, but higher cards can wait until you've built up the layout more and exposed as many face-down cards as you can.

Beleaguered Castle

♠ ♥ ♣ ♦ ♠ ♥ ♣ ♦

Can you break down the castle walls and win the battle?

1. Remove the four aces from the deck and place them in a non-overlapping column to begin your foundations. You will build up on these foundations in suit.

2. Next, deal eight rows of six face-up cards, with two rows on either side of each ace. This is your layout, and you should have no cards left over.

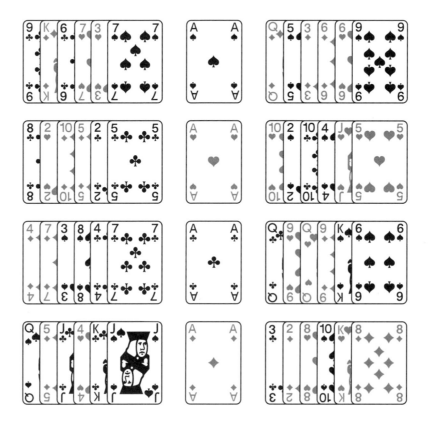

3. Notice how the layout cards overlap. Only the cards on top of a row (the eight cards without any cards covering them) can be played, and only one card at a time. No full or partial builds may be moved.

4. Build down on the layout rows, without regard to suit or color.

5. If you remove all the cards in a row, you may move any top card to the space this creates.

6. If you move all the cards to the foundations, you win!

strategy: Planning ahead is very important in this game, and you should never move cards around the layout only because you can. Just like a real castle siege, you should try to knock down the walls around the foundation. First try to remove all the cards from a row, so that you have a space. Don't build too high on any one foundation, since you might need some of those cards to build on in your layout. Try to build all four foundations together.

variation: For an easier game, allow yourself to move builds around the layout. For a more difficult game, only build on the layout in alternating colors.

Canfield

♠ ♥ ♣ ♦ ♠ ♥ ♣ ♦

One of the most popular solitaire games!

1. Deal a pile of thirteen face-down cards, and turn up the top card. This will be your reserve pile. Deal four cards face up to the right of this to form your layout.

2. Deal one face-up card just above your layout to form the first foundation. The rank of this card—jack, eight, two, or whatever— will be the rank used to begin the other three foundations. Move these other three cards next to your first foundation as they turn up during play.

reserve pile

3. Build up the foundations by suit, playing an ace on a king, and a two on an ace. The final card you place on a foundation pile will be one rank lower than the card that began each pile. For example, if your foundation pile begins with four, it is complete when it shows a three.

4. Build downward on the layout by alternating color, moving single cards or complete builds from one pile to another. Partial builds may not be moved.

5. If you remove all the cards from a pile, the space must be filled immediately with the top card from your reserve. If you've already played all the reserve cards, then you can fill a space anytime with any available card or build.

6. Once you've played all the cards you can from the layout and reserve, begin turning over cards in your stockpile three at a time. Don't deal them one after another, since this will change the order of the cards. Instead, take all three cards from the top of your pile and turn them over. This way, you will see the third card instead of the first card. If you can play the face-up card, you will expose the next card, which you can also play. The other two cards can be played only when they are exposed by playing the cards on top of them.

7. Place whichever cards you can't play into a wastepile, face up. Continue turning over cards three at a time from your stockpile and placing the unplayed ones face up onto your wastepile. You may play the top card of the wastepile or the reserve pile at any time during the game.

8. When you've gone all the way through the stockpile (you may be able to turn over only one or two cards when you reach the end of the stockpile), turn over your wastepile to form a new stockpile. Then continue taking three cards at a time from the stockpile.

9. Go through the stockpile as many times as you want in this way, until you can't play any more cards. Move all the cards to the foundations before this happens, and you're a winner!

strategy: Move cards to create spaces in the layout, and don't move too many cards to the foundations at one time. Make sure you've played all the cards you can *before* turning over another stack of three from your stockpile. Sometimes you'll only get to see a card from the stockpile once during a game before it gets buried beneath other cards.

variations: Here are some variations on this popular game:

Selective Canfield is the same in every way, except you deal five cards face up, just after setting aside your reserve. Four of these face-up cards will form your layout, and the other will begin the foundation piles. If you're lucky enough to deal out a pair (or if you form a pair with the top card of your reserve), make these your foundations. Otherwise, choose your layout cards to allow the most building.

Storehouse is an easier variation that allows you to remove the twos in the deck before beginning the game. These will begin your foundations.

Superior Demon allows you to deal the reserve pile in a face-up row and take any card from it at any time. You can also move partial builds and fill spaces in your layout with any available card at any time.

Klondike

♠ ♥ ♣ ♦ ♠ ♥ ♣ ♦

The most famous solitaire game of all

1. Deal a row of seven face-down cards to begin your layout. Then deal another row of six face-down cards on top of this, beginning with the second pile. Deal a row of five face-down cards on top of this, beginning with the third pile, and so on, until you have a pile each of one, two, three, four, five, six, and seven cards. Turn over the top card of each pile and square up your cards, and your layout is complete. The leftover cards form your stockpile.

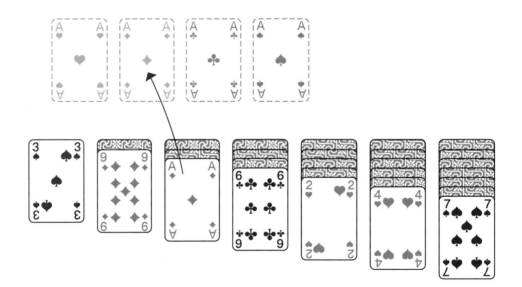

2. The foundations begin with aces, which are placed above the layout as they turn up during play. Build up on the foundations by suit.

3. Build down in the layout in alternating colors. You may move single cards or complete builds, but not partial builds. Turn over face-down cards when they are uncovered.

4. When you remove a pile of cards, the space may only be filled at first with a king, or with a build beginning with a king. Once all the kings are at the bottoms of piles or played to the foundations, you may fill empty spaces with any card or build.

5. After you have played all the cards you can in the layout, begin turning over the stockpile one card at a time, playing either to the layout or the foundations.

6. Cards that cannot be played are placed face up in the wastepile. The top card of the stockpile and wastepile can always be played. There is no redeal.

7. If you move all the cards to the foundations, you win!

strategy: Because only the aces <u>must</u> be played immediately to a foundation, you must choose between playing a card to the foundations, or building on the layout. Generally, build cards lower than a four to the foundations, but keep middle cards in the layout as long as possible. The highest cards should be built to foundations only late in the game. Always try to build to create spaces in the layout or to turn over face-down cards. When given the choice, play last from the stockpile: first move cards in the layout, and then play cards from the wastepile.

variations: Hundreds of variations on "Klondike" exist. Some variations allow you to turn over cards in your stockpile three at a time, as in "Canfield," or allow as many redeals as it takes for you to win. Others use only five piles in the beginning layout or allow you to always move one card (even if it's at the bottom of a build) or to move any partial builds. Most of these variations make the game easier to win. Here are a few popular ones:

Thumb and Pouch allows you many more chances to build on the layout, for a much easier game. The foundations are still built upward, but a card may be built (in the layout or foundations) on any suit *except* for its own suit. Full or partial builds may be moved, and spaces are filled with any available card or build.

Whitehead changes many things about "Klondike," and is almost a totally new game. Deal all the cards in the layout face up and build down in the layout by same color—red on red, black on black. The only builds that can be moved are complete builds of the same suit, so try to build down by suit wherever possible. Empty layout spaces may be filled with any available card or build.

Spiderette has the same layout as "Klondike," but you do not move cards to foundations. Build down in the layout without paying attention to suits, but keep in mind that only builds (full or partial) of the same suit can be moved, so build down by suit whenever you can. Turn over face-down cards that are uncovered, as in "Klondike," and fill spaces with any available card or movable build. When you've made all the moves you can, deal seven cards from the stockpile face up on all the piles. Do not play until all seven cards have been dealt. Continue in this way through the deck, without any wastepile. Move partial builds around the layout to uncover the cards beneath them. If you create a build from king to ace in the same suit, then you can move it to a foundation. If you remove all four suits this way, you win.

In **Two-Person Klondike**, two people can play at once with different decks. Pick decks that have different designs or colors on the backs, because you'll need to sort the cards later. Sit opposite each other and play two separate games of "Klondike" just as you normally would, except there are as many redeals as you want. Play onto your own layouts, and as you turn over aces, put them in the space between your layouts, and play other cards on top of them. You can play on each other's foundations. This means that if you're stuck, you can wait for your opponent to add a card to the foundation piles that will allow you to continue playing. When both of you try to put the same card on a foundation, the card on the bottom (the one that got there first) is the card that stays. When you are both stuck, separate the foundation piles into your two different decks. Count your cards; the person with the most cards wins. If you both get rid of all your cards, it's a tie and you're both winners!

Lots of Cards
and
Lots of Fun

♠ ♥ ♣ ♦ ♠ ♥ ♣ ♦

Basic
Two-Pack
Games

Contradance

♠ ♥ ♣ ♦ ♠ ♥ ♣ ♦

Dance with the fives and sixes as long as you can

1. Remove all the fives and sixes from the deck and place them in two rows as shown. These will be your foundations. Build up on the sixes in suit until you reach queens, and build down on the fives in suits until you reach kings, playing a king on an ace.

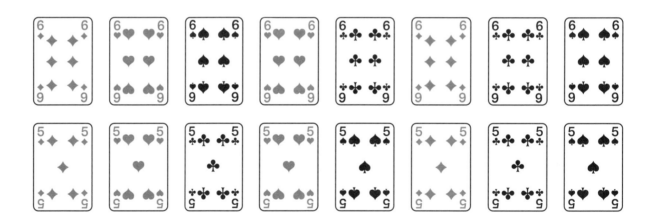

2. The rest of the cards are your stockpile. Turn over cards one at a time, and play them straight to the foundations. There is no layout in this game.

3. Put all unplayable cards face up onto a wastepile. You may play the top card from the wastepile at any time.

4. When you have gone through the stockpile once, redeal by turning over the wastepile to make a new stockpile. You may do this once.

5. If you dance your way through the deck and move all the cards to the foundations, you win!

Busy Aces

♠ ♥ ♣ ♦ ♠ ♥ ♣ ♦

Keep the aces—and all the cards—moving

1. Deal twelve face-up cards in two rows of six cards. Give yourself plenty of room between the rows, since you will be building below each row. The eight foundations, begun with aces and built up in suit, will be placed in a row above these cards. The remainder of the deck is your stockpile.

2. The layout is built down in suit by moving cards one at a time. Full and partial builds may not be moved.

3. Spaces created by moving an entire row can be filled from the top card of the stockpile or the wastepile, but not from within the layout.

4. Begin play by making whatever moves you can within the layout piles, then continue by turning over cards one at a time from your stockpile.

5. Unplayable cards are placed face up into a wastepile, the top card of which can be played at any time.

6. If you move all the cards to the foundation piles, you've been a busy little ace, and you win!

strategy: Whenever you have the choice of playing a card, play first from the layout (if this creates a space in the layout), then from the wastepile, and lastly from your stockpile. This gives you the most strategic opportunities, and makes sure you don't bury important cards in the wastepile.

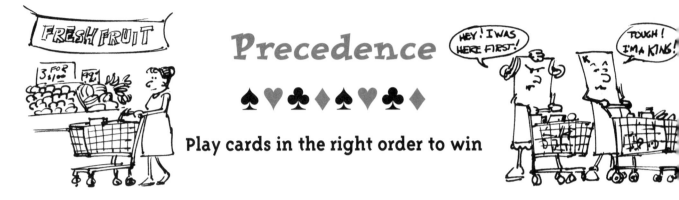

Precedence

♠ ♥ ♣ ♦ ♠ ♥ ♣ ♦

Play cards in the right order to win

1. Pull any king out of the deck to begin the first foundation. There will be eight foundations in all, each one beginning with a card of different rank and placed in descending order from left to right. So the next foundation to the right of the king will start with a queen, then the next pile will begin with a jack, and so on, down to six at the far right of the foundation row.

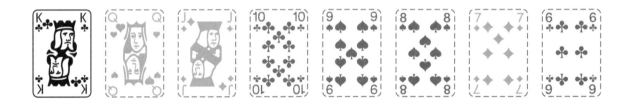

2. There is no other layout for this game. Go through your deck one card at a time and build down without paying attention to suit. Play whichever cards to the foundations that you can, but a new foundation cannot be started until all the foundations to its left have been started. The only foundation that can be started next, therefore, is the one beginning with the queen, just to the right of the king.

3. Once a foundation has begun, you may build on it as much as you want, until it reaches the card that is one rank higher than the card that began the foundation. So the foundation that began with a seven will end with an eight, for example, and every foundation will contain thirteen cards. Play kings on aces when necessary to continue building.

4. Continue to build down on each foundation in this way until you reach its ending card.

5. Place all unplayable cards face up in a wastepile. You may play the top card of the wastepile at any time.

6. You may redeal twice in this game. Just turn over the wastepile to make a new stockpile and continue the game.

7. If you move all the cards to the eight foundations, you win!

strategy: Beginning the foundations is the priority, so make those plays first. Unfortunately, this means that you will always begin a new foundation before beginning to build on the one just before it, which may seem to stop play for you. But it will pay off in the long run.

The only other choice in this game will be where to play some cards. Always play on the shortest foundation pile.

Snake

♠ ♥ ♣ ♦ ♠ ♥ ♣ ♦

A slithery, scaly, sneaky game

YOU CAN SEE
I'M NOT A
DIAMONDBACK!

1. Remove one card of each rank from the deck—suits don't matter. Arrange them into an S shape, with the seven at the bottom of the S (the snake's tail) and a six at the top (the snake's head). All the other cards in between should be in order, with the eight next to the seven, and so forth, with the ace played after the king.

2. These thirteen cards are your foundations, and there is no other layout. The rest of the cards will be your stockpile.

3. Build up on the foundations, without paying any attention to suit, until the seven at the tail reaches an ace, the eight reaches a two, and so on, up to the six, which will reach king. You may find it helpful to turn a completed foundation pile over (or sideways) so that you won't accidentally continue to play on it.

92 •

4. Go through the cards in your stockpile one at a time, playing directly to the foundations when you can.

5. Put unplayable cards on one of two wastepiles. You may play the top *two* cards from either of these piles at any point, so you may want to spread the piles out a little.

6. If you make a snake using all the cards, you win! There should be an ace at the tail, a king at the head, and all the cards in between in the right order.

variation: **Suit Snake** is a variation in which you can only build in a certain order of suits. Begin the game as in "Snake," except all the cards that begin your foundations must be diamonds. Build on these foundations in this suit order: diamonds, spades, hearts, clubs, then diamonds again.

order:

Unplayable cards are placed in one of four wastepiles, and you can use either of the top two cards of any pile at any time. Give yourself two redeals by picking up the wastepiles in any order and turning them over to make a new stockpile. If you complete "Suit Snake," the snake will have all clubs, ace to king, from tail to head.

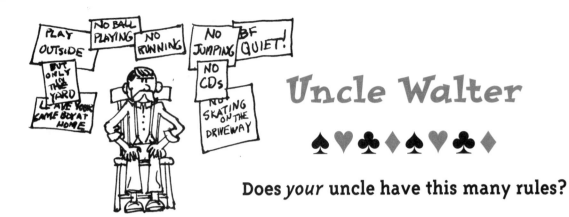

Uncle Walter

♠ ♥ ♣ ♦ ♠ ♥ ♣ ♦

Does *your* uncle have this many rules?

1. Deal twelve cards face up into four rows of three cards. These are your layout piles, and you will begin the foundations in a row above them, starting with aces. The rest of your cards make up your stockpile.

2. Build up in suit on the foundations and down in suit on the layout piles. You may move single cards, full or partial builds, but only when you are moving within the same row or to a higher row (see next page for examples).

3. When you create a space in the layout, immediately fill it with the top card of your wastepile or from the stockpile if the wastepile is empty.

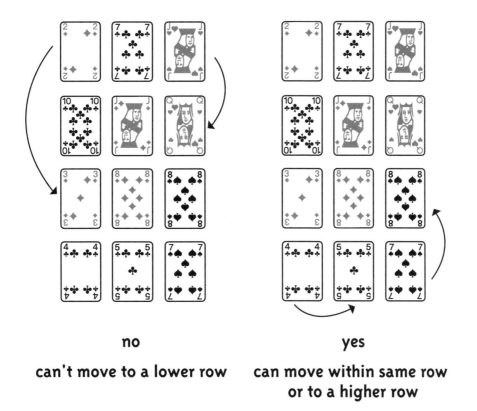

no

can't move to a lower row

yes

**can move within same row
or to a higher row**

4. After you have moved all the cards you can within the layout, begin turning over cards in your stockpile one at a time. Play these cards to the foundations or the layout piles, and place unplayable ones face up in a wastepile. The top card of the wastepile is available for play.

5. If you move all the cards to the foundations, you beat Uncle Walter!

strategy: When you have a choice of which card to play to a foundation, you should choose the card on the higher row most of the time, since that will leave you with more options for play.

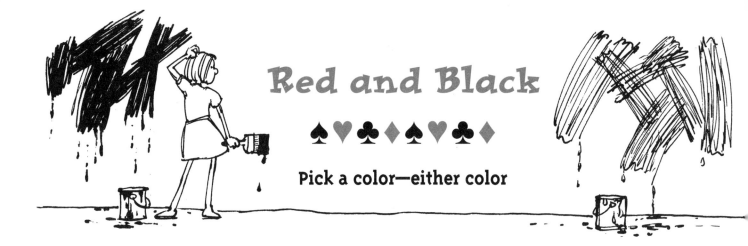

Red and Black

♠ ♥ ♣ ♦ ♠ ♥ ♣ ♦

Pick a color—either color

1. Take all eight aces from the deck and place them in a row to begin the foundations. They will be built up in alternate colors until you reach kings.

2. Deal a row of eight cards below these to finish the layout. The rest of the cards will be your stockpile.

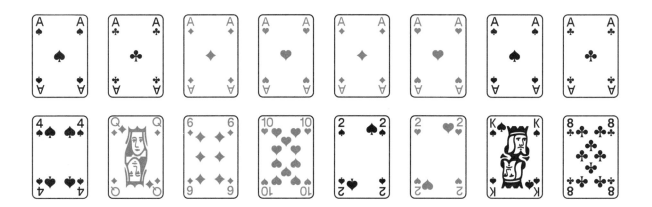

3. Build down in alternate colors on these layout piles, moving only one card at a time. Full and partial builds cannot be moved.

4. When a space is created in the layout by moving all the cards in a pile, fill it at once with the top card from your wastepile. If there is no wastepile, use the top card from your stockpile.

5. When you have made all the moves you can within the layout, begin turning over cards in the stockpile one at a time, playing either to the foundations or layout piles.

6. Place unplayable cards face up in a wastepile. The top card of the wastepile is available for play at any time.

7. You may redeal in this game once. Turn over the wastepile to begin a new stockpile and continue playing.

8. If you move all the cards to the foundations, you're a winner!

strategy: Unlike other building games, long builds are not a problem in this game, since they can easily (and sometimes instantly) be moved to the foundations. So build, build, build! Be careful when creating space, however. Wait until there's a high card on top of the wastepile, so that your building is not restricted by a low card.

variation: A harder game allows you to move full and partial builds in the layout, but there's no redeal.

Sly Fox

♠ ♥ ♣ ♦ ♠ ♥ ♣ ♦

Are you as clever as this game?

1. Remove four aces and four kings (one of each suit) from the deck. Put the aces in a column on the left and the kings in a column on the right, as shown. These will be your eight foundations. Build up on the aces in suit to kings, and build down on the kings in suit to aces.

2. Between your eight foundations, deal twenty face-up cards in four rows of five cards each. This completes your layout, and the rest of the cards will be your stockpile.

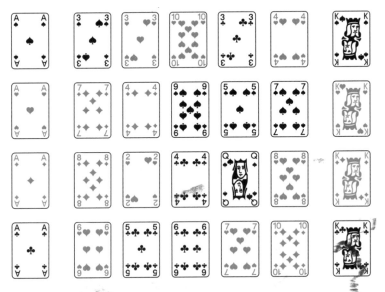

3. Play whatever cards you can from the twenty layout piles to the foundations. Fill in the spaces with the top card(s) of your stockpile.

4. After you have played what you can from the layout, begin going through the cards in your stockpile one at a time. Play what cards you can directly to the foundations. You may place the other cards on any one of the twenty layout piles, no matter how many cards are on that pile or what the top card is.

5. Once you've played twenty cards to the layout piles (don't count the ones you play directly to the foundations), stop going through the cards in your stockpile. Play any cards that you can from the layout piles, but not before this point!

6. After playing what you can, continue with the stockpile, as in step 4. Pause after twenty cards have been played to the layout piles to play whatever layout cards you can.

7. If you create spaces in the layout by removing all the cards in a pile (after the opening deal), fill these spaces the next time you go through the stockpile. Once a card is placed on a layout pile, it can only be moved to a foundation pile—not to a space or another layout pile.

8. Continue going through the stockpile in this way, without a redeal. If you move all the cards to the foundations, you're a sly fox.

strategy: Try to build up or down in suit when you can, so that the cards can be moved immediately to the correct foundation piles. Just be careful not to block yourself by burying important cards deep in a layout pile.

Intrigue

♠ ♥ ♣ ♦ ♠ ♥ ♣ ♦

Follow the queens to victory!

1. This game will take up a lot of space, so find a big table or use the floor. Pull any queen from the deck and place it in front of you. Begin dealing cards face up in a column on top of the queen, continuing until another queen is dealt.

2. Begin a new column with this second queen, dealing cards face up on top of it until a third queen is reached. Again, begin a new column with the queen, continuing in this way through the deck until all eight queens are at the top of eight columns, with the entire deck dealt out in the columns below them. The columns will be of very different lengths, and some may not have any cards below the queen at all. (See the sample layout on the following page.)

3. Remove all fives and sixes from the columns and place them in two rows above the eight columns. These will be your foundations. Build up on the sixes, without paying attention to suit, until you reach jacks. Build down on the fives, also without paying attention to suit, until you reach kings, which are played on aces.

SAMPLE LAYOUT

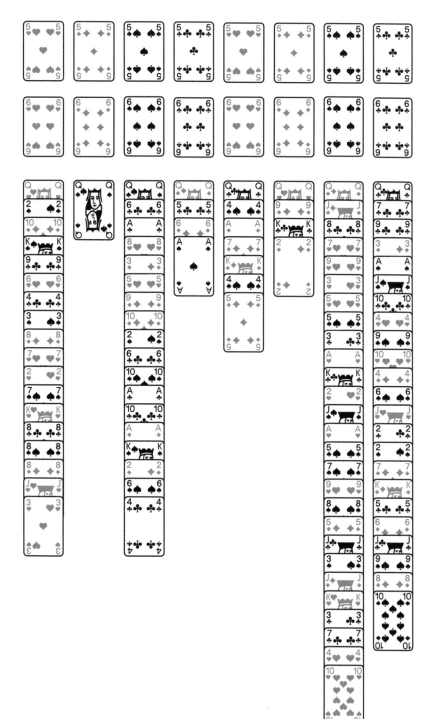

4. Build on the layout columns either up or down, regardless of suit. You may build in both directions on a single column, playing a seven on an eight, for example, and then playing either a six or an eight on this seven.

5. Only single cards are available for building. No full or partial builds may be moved.

6. When all cards have been removed from on top of a queen, you may move any available card to the top of the queen. Note that queens are not built to the foundations, so they are simply used to hold spaces in the layout.

7. If you move all of the cards to the foundations, you win!

strategy: You have a lot of flexibility in this game, both in the foundations and the layout piles, so you'll have many chances for strategic play. Plan your moves ahead, and try to build in one direction on a layout pile whenever possible. When you create a space, try to move either a jack or king there, since these will be played last on any foundation pile.

Lots of Fun
and
Lots of Skill

♠♥♣♦♠♥♣♦

Advanced
Two-Pack
Games

Grand Duchess

♠ ♥ ♣ ♦ ♠ ♥ ♣ ♦

What she plays when the Grand Duke is around

1. Deal a row of four face-up cards to create the layout, then deal two face-down cards to begin a reserve pile.

2. The eight foundations will be placed above this, in two rows. Four of the foundations begin with a king, one of each suit. The other four foundations begin with an ace, one of each suit. Move these cards up to the foundation piles as they become available. Build the kings down in suit until they reach aces, and build the aces up in suit until they reach kings.

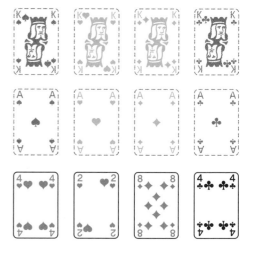

reserve
pile

3. The layout cards are only played onto the foundations and are not built on one another. Empty spaces are filled only with the next six-card deal, as explained on the next page.

4. When you have played what cards you can to the foundations, deal one face-up card to each of the piles and two more face-down cards to the reserve pile. Do not play any cards until all six cards have been dealt.

5. Continue playing and dealing like this (although your final deal may not add cards to every pile). When all the cards have been dealt, turn over the reserve pile and spread the cards out. You may play any cards from the reserve pile onto the foundations.

6. Once you have played all you can from the reserve pile, redeal by collecting all four layout piles from right to left, with the right pile on top. Add what is left of the reserve to the bottom of the stack, and deal six cards as in step 1, then continue playing as before.

7. You may redeal like this three times. On the last deal, deal all the cards to the layout, four at a time, and don't deal any cards to the reserve pile.

8. If you have moved all the cards to the foundation, you've won!

strategy: The main choice here is whether to play a particular card in the ace or king foundations. Play low cards to the ace foundations and high cards to the king foundations. The cards in the middle will depend on where you are in the game, but often it's just a lucky guess with these cards.

Ferris Wheel

♠ ♥ ♣ ♦ ♠ ♥ ♣ ♦

A game to make your head spin!

1. Deal twelve cards face up in three rows of four cards each. This will be your layout, and the rest of the cards are your stockpile. There are no foundations in this game.

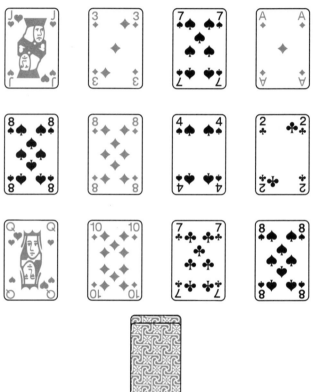

stockpile

2. The object of this game is to collect three number (non-face) cards that total eighteen, then pair those three cards with any face card. All four cards can then be discarded.

3. No set of number cards can be discarded if there is more than one card of the same rank. For example, a ten, six, and two can be matched with a face card and discarded, but a ten and two fours cannot. (See next page for more examples.)

4. Discard aces all by themselves, without matching to other cards. They cannot be used with other cards to total eighteen.

5. As spaces appear in the layout, fill them immediately with your stockpile. Cards in the stockpile are not otherwise used.

6. If you discard all the cards in the deck, you win!

strategy: Whenever more than one card of the same rank are in your layout, try to get rid of one of them. Otherwise you may end up being blocked when most of the cards in your layout are the same.

EXAMPLES OF CARDS THAT CAN BE DISCARDED AS SETS

yes

EXAMPLES OF CARDS THAT CANNOT BE DISCARDED AS SETS

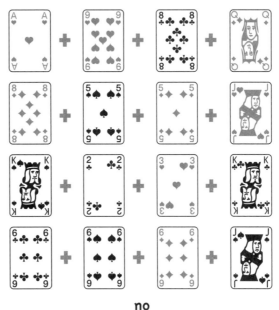

no

Windmill

♠ ♥ ♣ ♦ ♠ ♥ ♣ ♦

A game to keep you spinning and whirling

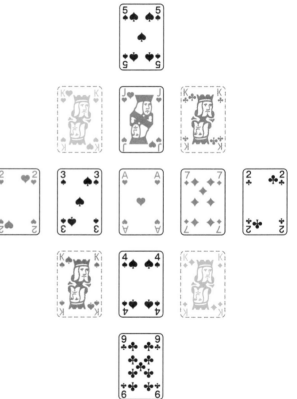

1. Take any ace from the deck and place it in the middle of your layout. Deal eight cards, two extending from each side of the ace, as shown. This is your layout, and the rest of the cards are your stockpile.

2. The ace is one of your foundations and will be built up without paying attention to suit, until it contains fifty-two cards. Build aces on kings, and continue until you've gone four times through the sequence of cards from ace to king.

3. The other four foundations begin with kings. As they turn up, put one foundation at each corner of the ace, as shown. Build down on these foundations, also without paying attention to suit, until you reach aces.

4. Play cards from the layout to the foundations, but do not build on layout piles. Replace them with the top card from your wastepile or from your stockpile, if the wastepile is empty.

5. When you have played all you can from the layout, turn over the cards in your stockpile one at a time. Play these directly to the foundations.

6. "Windmill" allows one kind of special play between foundations. If you need a card for the middle (ace) foundation that's on a king foundation, for example, you may take it. But the next card that you play on the ace foundation must come from the layout, wastepile, or stockpile.

7. You cannot move more than one card at a time from a king to an ace foundation, and there is no moving any cards from the ace foundation to any of the king foundations.

8. If you move all the cards to the foundations, you win!

strategy: The choice you'll be faced with is whether to play to the center ace foundation or the king foundations. Most of the time, you'll want to play to the ace foundation, since it will take the longest to build. There will be some exceptions to this, especially late in the game, but stick to this rule in general.

New York, New York

♠ ♥ ♣ ♦ ♠ ♥ ♣ ♦

The game so nice, they named it twice

1. Deal a row of eight face-up cards to begin the layout piles and a ninth card directly above this row to begin the foundations. All seven other cards of the same rank as this ninth card will begin the other foundations and should be moved up to the foundation row as they become available. The rest of the cards will be your stockpile.

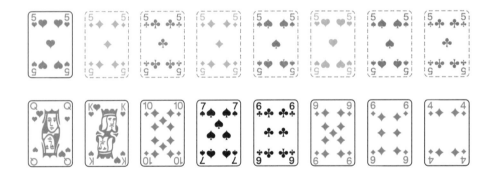

2. Build up on the foundations in suit until you reach the card one rank below the card that began the foundation piles. For example, if sevens begin all the foundation piles, each one should be built up to six. Play aces on kings, then twos on aces, when necessary.

3. Build down on the layout piles in alternating colors, moving only single cards. Full or partial builds may not be moved.

4. When you have played whatever cards you can in the layout, turn over cards one at a time from the stockpile. If you cannot play a card, place it on one of three wastepiles. The top card of any wastepile may always be played.

5. When you create a space by removing all of a layout pile, fill the space with any of the top cards in the three wastepiles. You do not need to fill a space immediately, so you can wait until a good card appears on a wastepile before moving it to a space.

6. If you move all the cards to the foundations, you're a winner!

strategy: The two secrets to success in this game involve using layout spaces properly, and paying attention to how you lay cards on the three wastepiles. Save one wastepile for high cards only, noting that high cards aren't necessarily face cards. High cards are those cards played last to the foundation piles, so if your foundations begin with threes, then aces and twos would be considered high cards.

When you can, build either down in suit (the opposite of foundation building) or up in alternating colors (the opposite of layout building) on your wastepiles. This way, you can move many cards quickly from the wastepiles to the layout or foundations.

Face cards should still be moved to spaces whenever possible, because layout cards are built down from them. There will be times, however, when playing other cards there will help open up more layout spaces or allow for longer builds.

Frog

♠ ♥ ♣ ♦ ♠ ♥ ♣ ♦

A two-pack game that will keep you hopping!

1. Deal thirteen cards face up to make a reserve pile. If any aces are in your reserve pile, use them to begin your foundation row, adding cards to replace them in the reserve so that the total is still thirteen. The rest of the cards will be your stockpile.

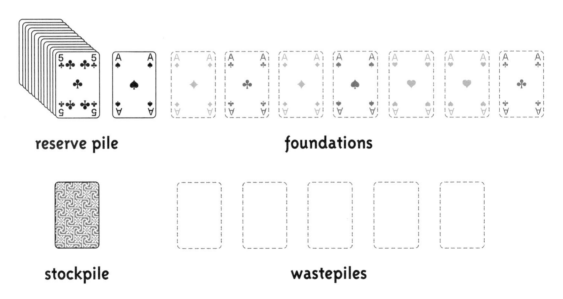

reserve pile   foundations

stockpile   wastepiles

2. If no aces come up in the reserve pile, remove one from the stockpile and place it to begin your foundation row. The other aces will be moved to this row as they become available, then built up on without paying attention to suit or color.

3. Turn over the cards in your stockpile one at a time, playing them to the foundations when you can. You may play the top card of your reserve to the foundations at any time.

4. Put any cards you cannot play into one of five wastepiles. The top card of each of these wastepiles is available at any time, so the order of each wastepile is very important.

5. There is no building in this game. If you eliminate a wastepile, you can only fill the space with the top card from your stockpile.

6. If you have moved all the cards to the foundations, you're Top Frog, and you've won!

strategy: Pay attention to where you place your discards in the wastepiles. Use one pile for face cards, and try to build down on others whenever possible. Try to set yourself up so that when one card is played to a foundation, you will be able to follow it up with many more. Whenever possible, avoid putting a card—or a series of cards—on top of cards of lower rank. Doing this too often will bury these cards and make them impossible to retrieve.

Deauville

The city of great card games

1. Deal thirty cards into ten face-down columns of three cards each. Turn over the top card of each column. The eight foundations will be placed in a row above these thirty cards and built up in suit from ace. The rest of the cards will be your stockpile.

2. Build down in the layout in alternating colors, moving only single cards. Full and partial builds may not be moved.

3. Move cards to the foundations as they become available, either from your stockpile or from the layout.

4. Turn over face-down cards in the layout when they are exposed.

5. Spaces created in the layout are filled with any card from the layout, or the top card of the wastepile or stockpile.

6. Turn over cards one at a time from your stockpile when you cannot make any more moves in the layout. Stockpile cards may be built on the layout cards or the foundation piles.

7. Put any unplayable cards on a wastepile, face up. The top card of the wastepile is always available.

8. Move all the cards to the foundation piles and you win!

strategy: As in "Klondike," the central strategy here involves deciding when to move a card to the foundations. Move low cards immediately to foundations, and hold on to high cards to build on. Try not to create too many builds on middle cards, however—otherwise, important cards will be buried. Build up all foundations as equally as possible.

Carlton

♠ ♥ ♣ ♦ ♠ ♥ ♣ ♦

It's tons of fun!

1. Deal a row of eight face-up cards. Deal seven face-up cards on top of these, overlapped so that you can read the cards underneath, and skipping the last pile on the right. Deal six face-up cards on these, skipping the last two piles, and continue in this way with five, four, three, two, and one face-up card.

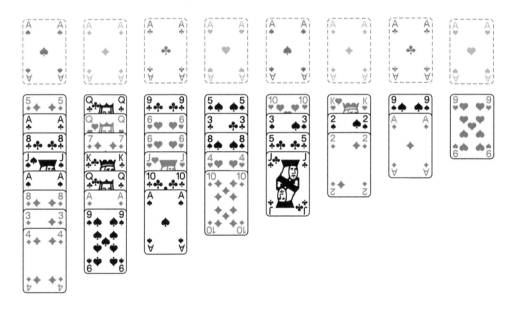

You should have eight face-up columns when you are finished, one column each of eight, seven, six, five, four, three, two, and one card. This is your layout, and the eight foundations will be placed in a row above this, built up in suit, beginning with aces.

2. Build down on the layout, without paying attention to suit or color. You may move single cards as well as full and partial builds. Move cards one at a time to the foundations as they turn up.

3. Spaces created in the layout are filled from the layout only, by moving a single card or a full or partial build to the space.

4. When you can't make any more moves in the layout, deal one card onto the top card of each column in the layout (the bottom of the column) and continue playing. Do not make any moves until all eight cards have been dealt this way.

5. If you can move all the cards onto the foundations, you're a winner!

strategy: This game is similar to both "Klondike" and its variation, "Spiderette," and uses many of the same strategies. Aces are the only cards that must be moved to the foundations, so it's sometimes important to keep cards in your layout to build on them. Generally speaking, low cards can be moved quickly to foundations, but higher cards should be held in the layout. Try to build all foundation piles as equally as possible. Also, try to make moves in the layout that free up spaces, as this gives you the most options. Finally, make sure you've made all the moves you can before dealing the next eight cards.

Constitution

♠ ♥ ♣ ♦ ♠ ♥ ♣ ♦

We, the People, love this game!

1. Take all the kings, queens, and aces out of the deck. Discard the queens and kings and put the aces in a single row. The aces will begin the foundations and are built up in suit until they reach jacks.

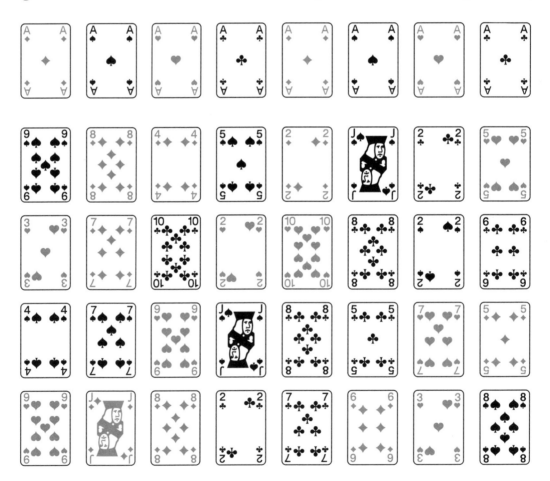

2. Deal thirty-two cards below the eight aces, in four rows of eight, as shown on the opposite page. This is your layout, and the rest of the cards will be your stockpile.

3. Cards may only be moved to the foundation from the top row of the layout. The cards in the top row of the layout are also the only cards that may be built upon. Build down on them in alternating colors, using only other cards in the top row or any of the cards in the second row. Build only with single cards. Full or partial builds may not be used.

4. Fill spaces in any row, including the top row, by moving a card up from the row directly beneath it. You may move any card up in that row, however, not just the one directly beneath the space. In the top row, spaces can be filled only with cards from the second row and not cards built on other cards in the first row.

5. When a space is created, move cards up as in step 4 one row at a time until you are left with a space in the bottom row. Fill this space with the top card from the stockpile. Make sure to fill spaces one row at a time, so that all the spaces in one row have been filled before moving cards from the row beneath it.

6. Cards from the stockpile may only be played to the layout and not to the foundations. So, if you cannot make a space in the layout and cannot play any cards to the foundations, the game is over.

strategy: It's important to plan ahead in this game and move cards that you need from the bottom rows. First, of course, you will want to move up low cards that you can play to the foundations. Then, move high cards that you can build on or cards that will continue builds.

Create spaces with building so that you can move cards. Plan builds in advance, moving cards up to the second row so that you can create long builds quickly, but don't make long builds on cards that you will need soon, since long builds can be very hard to remove. Build up all foundations as equally as possible.

Grand Canyon

♠ ♥ ♣ ♦ ♠ ♥ ♣ ♦

One of the seven wonders of the solitaire world

1. Deal twenty cards face up in two rows of ten cards each. These will be the layout piles, which work like wastepiles, as you'll see in step 5. The rest of the cards will be your stockpile.

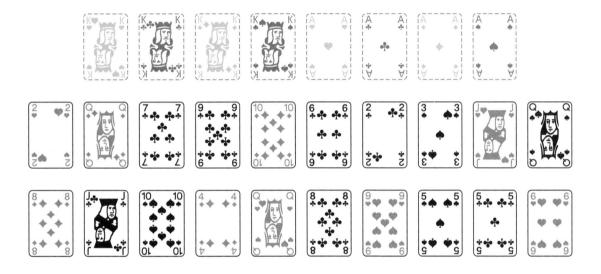

2. The eight foundations will be placed in a row above the layout. Four of the foundations begin with a king, one of each suit. You will build the kings down in suit until they reach aces. The other four foundations begin with an ace, one of each suit. Build these piles up in suit until they reach kings. Move cards up to the foundation piles as they become available.

3. The layout piles are played directly to the foundations, but are not built on one another.

4. When you have played all the cards that you can from the layout piles, begin turning over cards from your stockpile, one at a time.

5. If a card can be played to a foundation, you may play it. Otherwise, the card is placed on whichever one of the twenty layout piles you choose. Each card from the stockpile must either be played to a foundation or layout pile. There is no wastepile other than the twenty layout piles.

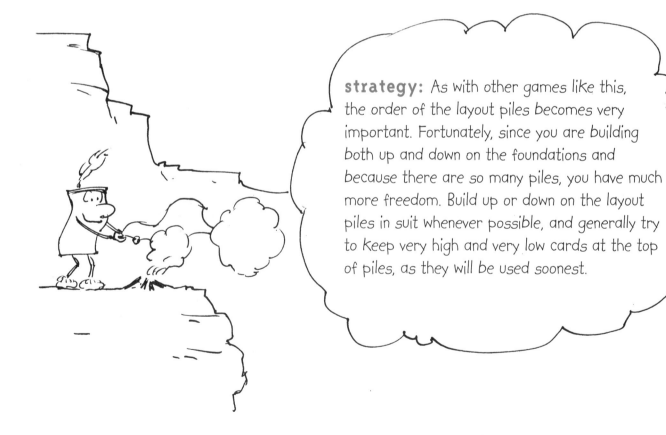

strategy: As with other games like this, the order of the layout piles becomes very important. Fortunately, since you are building both up and down on the foundations and because there are so many piles, you have much more freedom. Build up or down on the layout piles in suit whenever possible, and generally try to keep very high and very low cards at the top of piles, as they will be used soonest.

6. Empty spaces in the layout are filled immediately from the stockpile, not from other layout piles.

7. If you can move all the cards to the eight foundations, you've made it through the Grand Canyon and you're a winner!

The other choice you will have is whether to build up or down with a particular card. This choice will not come that often, but is usually important. High cards should generally be used to build on the kings, and low cards should be used to build on the aces. Where you play middle cards will depend on what your other layout piles look like. Choose the direction (up or down) that you will be able to continue soonest.

CONGRESS IS NOW IN SESSION!

WHO BR... THE C...

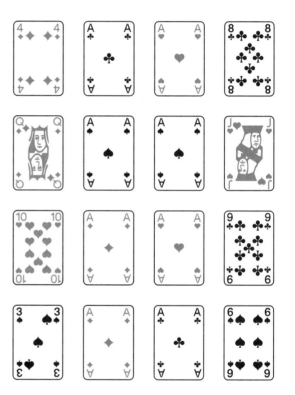

1. Remove all eight aces from the deck and place them in two columns to begin the foundations. Deal eight cards face up into two nonoverlapping columns on either side of the foundation rows, as shown. The rest of the deck is your stockpile.

2. Turn over the top card of your stock to begin a wastepile before beginning the game. The top card of both the wastepile and stockpile are always available.

3. The foundations are built up in suit, while the eight layout cards are built down, paying no attention to suit or color.

4. Cards may be moved only one at a time in the layout. No full or partial builds may be moved.

5. Spaces in the layout (created by removing all the cards in one of the eight piles) must be filled first with the top card of the wastepile. If there are no cards in the wastepile, the top card of the stock is used. Layout cards may only be used to fill spaces once the stockpile and wastepile are empty.

6. Turn over your stockpile one card at a time when all the moves in the layout and wastepile have been made. No redeals are allowed.

7. If you've moved all the cards to the foundations, you're a member of Congress and you've won!

strategy: Because the top card of the wastepile must *be* used to fill a space, don't create a space until you have an important card to play from the wastepile. Simply taking a card from the top of the stockpile to fill a space isn't smart, since you won't know what the card is until it has been played. Just keep turning over stockpile cards until a good one comes up. Knowing when to do this, and how many cards to turn over before settling for a less important card, is the most important part of this game. Turn over too many cards and the game will end early, or you may end up burying important cards.

Good cards to use in layout spaces are generally low cards or cards that can *be* used to continue a build. High cards can block layout spaces, since long builds are hard to make and even harder to take apart.

variation: An easier version of "Congress" allows a player to peek at the top card of the stockpile before deciding which card to play to a space or just to keep the stockpile face up, so the top card is always visible.

Parliament is a much more difficult version of this game, although the only difference is that the aces are not pulled out at the beginning. Just play them to the foundations when they become available.

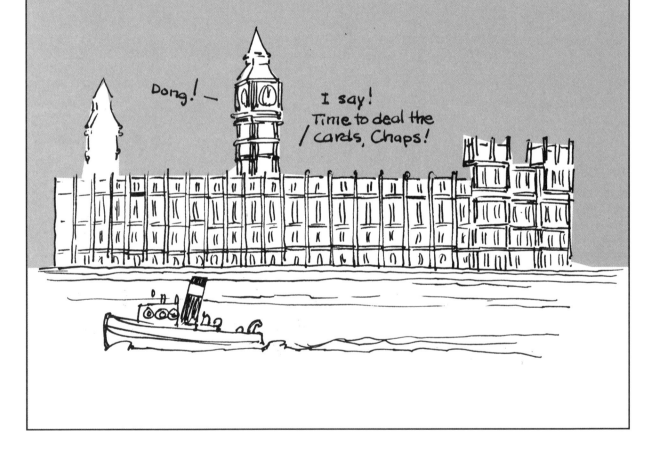

Glossary

build—A set of two or more cards that are arranged according to the building rules of the game. The top of a build is the only card without other cards covering it and is where any further cards can be added, while the bottom of a build is the card upon which all the other cards in a build are placed.

building—Creating a sequence of cards, usually in order of rank, according to the rules of a particular game. Kinds of building (often combined):

building by color—Building up or down by adding a card of the same or opposite (alternate) color.

building by suit—Building up or down by adding a card of the same suit to another.

building down—Adding a card that is one rank lower than the card below it.

building up—Adding a card that is one rank higher than the card below it.

column—A vertical line of cards, usually spread out so that the ranks of all the cards in the pile can be read.

complete build—An entire row or column of correctly built cards, which usually cover a pile or a space in the layout.

discard pile—A special pile where discards or cards from the stockpile that cannot be used again in the game are placed.

face cards—The jack, queen, and king of each suit, called this because they are the only cards in the deck with faces on them.

foundation—Special piles of cards, often in a row, usually built up by suit, that are the final destination of all cards in the game.

layout—The initial setup of all the cards in the game. These are often complicated and beautiful and sometimes change shape during the game.

partial build—Two or more cards at the top of a complete build that may be moved in some games.

pile—A squared-off stack of cards, usually all face down or face up.

rank—The value of a card, usually ascending from ace to ten, followed by jack, queen, and king. Some games allow aces to be played on kings (or vice versa) to continue a build. In solitaire games based on numbers, the card's rank determines its value—most often, jacks are valued as eleven, queens as twelve, kings as thirteen, and aces as one.

redeal—A way of continuing the game, usually accomplished by turning over the wastepile to create a new stockpile. The layout cards are sometimes collected, too; and in either case, the cards are not usually shuffled.

reserve—A special pile of cards, separate from layout and stockpile, that usually must be used before cards are drawn from the stockpile.

row—A horizontal line of cards, sometimes overlapped so that the rank of all the cards in the line can be seen.

square up—To align a pile of cards on all four sides, instead of overlapping cards in a column.

stockpile—A special face-down pile, not used in every game, usually made up of the cards left over after the layout has been created. These cards are used to continue the game, fill layout spaces, play to the foundations, or some combination of these.

suit—One of four symbols (hearts, diamonds, clubs, spades) used to mark and organize cards. A complete deck of cards will have one card of every rank in each suit. Two suits are red (hearts and diamonds) and two are black (spades and clubs), which is important in some solitaire games.

wastepile—A special pile, often face up, composed of cards from the stockpile that cannot be used yet. A redeal is often accomplished simply by turning over the wastepile to make a new stockpile. The top card of a wastepile is usually available for play.